DIRT, MESS AND D

DIRT, MESS AND DANGER

Liturgies & worship resources

Glendon Macaulay

wild goose publications

www.ionabooks.com

Compilation copyright © 2011 Glendon Macaulay
Contents © the individual contributors

First published 2011, reprinted 2013

Wild Goose Publications
4th Floor, Savoy House, 140 Sauchiehall Street, Glasgow G2 3DH, UK
www.ionabooks.com
Wild Goose Publications is the publishing division of the Iona Community.
Scottish Charity No. SC003794. Limited Company Reg. No. SC096243.

ISBN 978-1-84952-068-3

Cover illustration: 'The Word is made flesh (left side of a cross)',
from the 'Original Blessing' series © Ruth Goodheir

The publishers gratefully acknowledge the support of the Drummond Trust,
3 Pitt Terrace, Stirling FK8 2EY in producing this book.

A catalogue record for this book is available from the British Library.

Overseas distribution:
Australia: Willow Connection Pty Ltd, Unit 4A, 3-9 Kenneth Road,
Manly Vale, NSW 2093
New Zealand: Pleroma, Higginson Street, Otane 4170, Central Hawkes Bay
Canada: Novalis/Bayard Publishing & Distribution, 10 Lower Spadina Ave.,
Suite 400, Toronto, Ontario M5V 2Z2

Printed by Bell & Bain, Thornliebank, Glasgow

CONTENTS

INTRODUCTION

The church is one of the few places today where people are still told what they should know by the man or woman standing at the front. Go into any classroom in this country and you'll be hard-pressed to find a traditional lecture being delivered. Instead, children (and adults) are now more familiar with learning and discovering for themselves through the creation of opportunities for personal engagement, experience, experimentation and discourse with each other. A sermon as a vehicle of communication is therefore foreign to a great many folk, though the church doesn't seem to have quite cottoned on to that yet, since in many places the sermon is understood to be the only possible option for preaching the Word. Add to this a general reduction in individual and collective attention span, possibly encouraged by television screens whose images change every few seconds, and it is difficult to understand why alternative or complementary methods of communicating are not embraced more enthusiastically by worship leaders.

There's more than one way to tell a story. Most of the material in this collection attempts to enable worshippers to engage directly and actively in participative worship. Consequently, many of the prayers contain either spoken or sung responses, while others are intended to capture and maintain the attention of the congregation by virtue of their being led by several voices. The guided meditations are an attempt to encourage direct personal engagement between individuals and their God, while a feature of the more reflective items is imaginative scene-setting which leads individuals to places or scenarios where private and intimate conversations can take place. There are a few sermons, and a few blueprints for services in which a variety symbolic actions can be introduced.

Congregations are peculiar creatures who respond with an almost involuntary, knee-jerk reaction to any deviation from the hymn-prayer sandwich diet they have fed on for years – or so the rumour goes. I can honestly say I have never once found that to be the case when using the type of material contained in this book. Where more creative forms of worship are introduced sensitively, contextually and with integrity, these can be hugely effective in provoking, stimulating and enriching personal soul-searching. The underlying intention has always been that, at the end, more than one worshipper is able to leave saying: 'Today, in this very place, I came face-to-face with my God.'

I am very grateful to my good friend Rev Sally Foster-Fulton for allowing me to include some of her material in this collection, some of which has been adapted. Sally has an intense interest in the use of storytelling in worship. She is highly successful in using her own literary abilities and inventiveness to write imaginative material which draws the hearer into the events being described.

There are other people who ought to be thanked too, for their encouragement, enthusiasm and willingness to spend long hours proofreading, amending, correcting and making alternative (and much better) suggestions: Elizabeth Donald, John Miller and Jane Reid are members of Erskine Parish Church in Falkirk. Each of them has a great feel for language. I am very grateful to them.

Glendon Macaulay

ADVENT AND CHRISTMAS

WHEN LOVE WAS BORN

Can be sung to the tune 'Highwood' (CH4 246)

When Love was born, not all the earth cried 'Glory!'
Few realised, and fewer still were there.
Yet Love, undaunted, births a new conception:
the heart of heaven now present on the earth.

When Love was born: for space, a new dimension;
for time, the One who laughs and smiles and cries.
No more the strangeness of this place called heaven:
no longer distant God, who welcomes life.

When Love was born, the fear of God the Father
becomes the friendship found in Christ, the Son.
And, with the Spirit, laughing, celebrating,
divinity shouts: 'Come and join my dance!'

When Love was born, embracing human being,
not holding back from what it means to be,
Goodness in person brings earth hope and promise:
a bud unfolds even on the darkest day.

When Love was born, God enters our condition:
transforms what was, and is, and yet might be.
This is heaven's work, its passion and intention:
love, life and laughter for humanity.

LET US GO EVEN UNTO BETHLEHEM

The pace of this meditation needs to be taken very slowly throughout, with plenty of pauses for individuals to form their own mind-picture of the scene being described, and for personal reflection on the questions being asked. Before you begin, ask people to have the words of 'Child in the manger' (CH4 314) at hand.

Close your eyes, and let your mind go even unto Bethlehem to see in yonder manger low. Let your mind go to work, and imagine the place where this great thing has come to pass. The picture we are most likely to have is a romantic one – the reality was probably nothing like any of us might think. But let the traditional stable scene be sufficient for now, and let us imagine we are there, looking on at the birth of God.

The city is very quiet, the sky is very dark, the labour and the shouting are finished. From where you are standing, what does this stable look like?

- How big or how small is it?
- Is the atmosphere very cold in the bleak midwinter, or is it pleasant and comfortable, warmed by the breath of the animals?
- Is there straw on the floor, or is the bare earth covered in squelchy, smelly dung?
- Are there oil lamps dotted here and there to provide soft and restful light, or is there hardly any light at all?
- Is this really a stable, or is it a shed or a cave hollowed out of the rock?
- And what about the animals?
- Can you see the tired little donkey Mary rode on?
- Is there an ox, or maybe more than one, and are they lowing as cattle do?
- How many shepherds have left their sheep, having rushed from the hillside to be here? Count them now.

Of course, there are no kings here yet. They will visit later.

- But is that the innkeeper's wife?
- Was she the one who rolled up her sleeves and shouted: 'Push hard, girl! Push!' to help Mary through a painful delivery?
- Did she hold the mother's hand when the contractions were at their worst?
- Did she bring hot water when it was needed?
- Did she provide swaddling clothes for the baby?

- What is the baby wearing right now?
- And where is Joseph? What is he doing?
- And what about Mary?
- What age is she?

The baby is in the manger.

- Does he have hair, and if so, what colour and how much?
- Are his eyes closed or open?
- Is he girny and restless – hungry for his first feed from his mother's breast?
- Or is he placid and content, love smiling from his face?
- Little Jesus, sweetly sleep.
- Look at the baby's face now.

(Pause)

Look at his face.

- Exactly how has this baby, born so long ago, affected and influenced and shaped your life, and helped to shape the person you now are?
- How much of the pattern of your days – the things you do, the involvements you have, the groups you belong to – how much of that is directly due to this child and his birth?
- And what about your relationships? What about the way you interact with other people (family, friends, colleagues), the way you try to be decent and reasonable towards them, the way you feel it is right to share what you have and be generous? How much of this is due to having heard about this particular love child; this child of love so many have chosen to call their God?
- How much of it is because of this baby?

(Pause)

- So should you say how grateful you are for the way he has made you 'you'?
- If you had the courage to move closer, and tell him how much you owe him, and silently speak of your gratitude, and kneel beside the shepherds, what would you say?
- What would you say?
- What would you say?

A time of quiet

One voice begins to sing 'Child in the manger', and others join in.

ON THIS NIGHT OF NIGHTS

Voice 1:

Beyond our wildest imagining;
outwith the scope of our cleverest knowing;
escaping the farthest reach of our best understanding:
the Spirit of God, God of great power,
who cannot be harnessed.

Voice 2:

And yet this is the God we have come to speak with;
to listen and come close to,
to worship in this place and on this night.

Voice 3:

Be very careful as you make your approach.
Think carefully and think twice.
Because on this night of all nights,
at this time of all times,
the power of God is unleashed on an unsuspecting world.

Voice 1:

Think carefully and think twice,
because on this night of all nights,
at this time of all times,
you have come to worship the power
of a weak and helpless baby.

Voice 2:

Is this not the strangest thing we say,
the oddest and most unlikely thing to believe:
that a baby is, in fact, a God;
that an infant has such power;
that a child, born long ago,
has changed the world?

Voice 3:

Unless, of course, in weakness there is power.
Unless, of course, power can reside in weakness.

Voice 1:

Be very careful as you make your approach.
For on this night of all nights,
at this time of all times,
the power of God is unleashed upon the world.

Voice 2:

The weakness of this baby may change you.
You may find you are never the same again.

Voice 3:

Like the angels, we have come here to worship this weak child.
With the angels we will worship this most powerful God.

THE GOD OF HEAVEN IS COMING TO STAY

Song: 'Over my head, I hear music in the air' (chorus only, CH4 575)

Voice 1:

The stage is set:
the preparations are complete.
Heaven and earth come together on this sacred night.
The angels' song announces the time has finally come.
The longing earth is waiting for its God to be faithful
and keep the promise he has made.

Song: 'Over my head ...'

Voice 2:

Now God enters humanity:
becomes one with his people;
dwells within them and among them and beside them.
Divinity takes on human form,
and remains for ever with the folk he loves and treasures.

Song: 'Over my head ...'

Voice 1:

From the safety of a hidden place,
from the security of a secret place,
from the comfort of a mysterious place,
Love divine is born
to heal and hallow the whole human race.
Now is the moment – here is the place, this is the time
when we celebrate again
that Love has come
to make all things new.

Song: 'Over my head ...'

Voice 2:

Together like this,
let us worship the God of all,
and prepare to welcome the Christ child among us.
Together like this,
let us join in the music that fills the air
and celebrate that the God of heaven is coming;
that the God of heaven is coming to stay.

Song: 'Over my head ...'

VENI IMMANUEL

Song: 'Veni Immanuel' (*Come All You People*)

Voice 1:

Come, Immanuel,
for here is where heaven and earth come together in meeting.
Come and keep your appointment with us –
to let the power of your story affect us,
the reality of your presence touch us,
and the unity of our worship wrap us up
in sacred togetherness of heavenly, earthly love.

Song: 'Veni Immanuel'

Voice 2:

Come, Immanuel.
We will welcome you among us this Christmas time.
Come in the weakness of a baby
who has the power to melt our hearts to love;
to amend our thinking to generosity and compassion;
to change our experience and meaning and purpose
in all of our living on earth.

Song: 'Veni Immanuel'

Voice 3:

Come, Immanuel.
The world is in great pain.
Come bringing light and lightness to our living.
Come as welcome company for the lonely and hurting.
Come as forgiveness for the guilty and calming for the tormented.
Come disturbing the apathetic and upsetting the indifferent.
Come bringing peace and affirmation
for those who can find no peace within themselves.

Song: 'Veni Immanuel'

Voice 1:

Come, Immanuel.
Your world is ready; your people are waiting.
Come where hope is sleeping.
Come where faith has given way to fear.
Come where spirits long to leap again.
Come where joy is absent and tears are waiting to be dried.

Song: 'Veni Immanuel'

Voice 3:

Come, Immanuel.
Shape our living and our being.
Come and bless us
so that as we are blessed we will bless other people.
Come, Child of God, our best friend and companion.
Come, great hope of humanity.
Come to one and come to all on this holy night.

Song: 'Veni Immanuel'

GLORIA IN EXCELSIS

Song: 'Gloria in excelsis Deo' (Gloria 1 or 2, *Come All You People*)

Voice 1:

God-with-us!
You have come to bring reconciliation
in places where there is difference and division.
You have come to bring peace to summit meetings
where decisions are made for rifles to be loaded,
and rockets to be fired, and landmines to be laid.
You have come to challenge the quest of those who seek power.
God-with-us! Gloria in excelsis Deo!

Song: 'Gloria in excelsis Deo'

Voice 2:

God-with-us!
You have come to bring fairness to discussions
where generosity and compassion are absent,
and deals are struck only for profit or gain.
You have come to conversations and debates
that are motivated by selfishness and self-interest,
and where justice is seldom mentioned or never heard.
God-with-us! Gloria in excelsis Deo!

Song: 'Gloria in excelsis Deo'

Voice 3:

God-with-us!
You have come to homes where once-loving relationships have soured.
You have come to where one-time lovers
refuse to speak and now lead separate lives.
You have come to bedrooms where teenagers sit alone,
because communication has become awkward or too difficult.
You have come to young and old,
loved and unloved alike.
God-with-us! Gloria in excelsis Deo!

Song: 'Gloria in excelsis Deo'

Voice 4:

God-with-us!
You have come to living rooms
where widowers and widows are on their own this night.
You have come to where Christmas is no more than another working day.

Song: 'Gloria in excelsis Deo'

Voice 1:

God-with-us!

Voice 2:

You have come to mothers
who have no milk in their breasts to feed their babies.

Voice 3:

You have come to fathers
who sweat in labour for hardly any pay.

Voice 4:

You have come for the children
who simply don't know where their next mouthful will come from.

Voice 1:

You have come for those who do not care

Voice 2:

and will not lift a finger,

Voice 3:

and who look the other way.

You have come to all of your people.
You have come, and you are here, and here to stay.

Voice 4:

God-with-us!
You have come!
Christ is born!

Voices 1, 2, 3, 4:

Gloria in excelsis Deo!

Song: 'Gloria in excelsis Deo'

ONCE UPON A TIME

Voice 3 needs to be read by a woman, and Voice 4 by a young male.

Voice 1:

Once upon a time, there were two brothers, aged 8 and 10, who were inclined to get up to all kinds of mischief. Whenever anything went wrong, you could reckon it would turn out they had had a hand in it.

Voice 2:

Like the day all the wheelie bins in Thompson Crescent were set on fire. Nobody could prove it had anything to do with them, right enough, but Robert and James had been spotted lurking in the vicinity just about the time when the first call was put through to the fire brigade.

Voice 3:

Another time, a woman in Park Drive went to put away her watering can in the garden shed. She opened the door – and nearly had a heart attack when no less than five screeching cats jumped out, and then scattered in all directions at top speed. Again, nobody knew for sure who did it, but one of the brothers had been seen earlier in the day struggling with a cat tucked firmly under his arm.

Voice 4:

About 8 o'clock on Christmas Eve, in a block of flats, there was a knock on an old-age pensioner's door. She tried to open it, but it wouldn't budge. Little did she know that the handle of her door had been tied with a piece of clothes rope to the door handle of the flat on the opposite side of the landing, and that the person inside that flat was also frantically attempting to get out. By the time the woman had figured out what was wrong, and phoned her son-in-law to come and untie the rope, the criminals, whoever they were, were long gone.

Voice 1:

The boys' parents were at the end of their tether. It didn't matter what punishment they imposed – pocket money suspended, grounding the boys, making them wash the dishes by hand every night instead of allowing them to load up the dishwasher – it didn't seem to make one blind bit of difference. The duo continued to aggravate and upset the whole community with their pranks and monkey business.

Voice 2:

The new youth worker attached to the local churches believed she had a way with semi-delinquent children, so she made arrangements to meet up with James, the younger one. She thought she'd try an old trick. She'd frighten him into behaving himself by telling him that God was everywhere – and that God knew absolutely every-thing he and his brother got up to. After delivering what she believed to be an effective lecture, she pointed her finger at James and asked:

Voice 3:

'Where is God?'

Voice 2:

expecting the answer: 'Everywhere.' But James said nothing.

Voice 4:

She asked him again, in an even louder voice, but again James refused to answer. And so she tried for a third time, with her finger held right up to his nose:

Voice 3:

'Where is God?'

Voice 2:

But by that point, James was in a panic, and without saying a word, he suddenly jumped up and ran off home to talk to his brother, Robert.

Voice 4:

'Listen!' he said. 'We've really done it this time. We're in great big trouble.'

Voice 1:

'What do you mean we're in great big trouble?' asked his brother. 'We haven't done anything.'

Voice 4:

'Well,' gasped James, 'this woman kept on asking me if I knew where God is. Apparently God has gone missing – and we're getting the blame for it!'

Voice 2:

God has gone missing? Where is God? Well tonight, we have the answer to those questions, and we know for sure it has nothing at all to do with those two boys who, for once, are completely innocent.

- For on this night of all nights, we don't need to wonder any more where God is, or who God is, or where we will find him.

- On this night of all nights, God is no longer elusive; absent from sight, or silent in sound.

- On this night of all nights, God is present; God is active; God is known to be living.

- For the truth of it is this: God is flesh of our flesh, bone of our bone, for Love has come down.

Voice 1:

If the youth worker had asked me, I could have told her where God most definitely is *not*.

- Despite what the ever-so-cute little children have been singing for the past few weeks, God is not 'Away in a manger', confined for ever to a two-thousand-year-old historical past in some stable near Bethlehem.

- I could have assured her God is not some old guy with a beard sitting on a cloud high up in the sky, taking some well-deserved R&R, and enjoying the music of a company of angels, all of whom happen to be really good singers in a well-rehearsed choir.

- And maybe she would have been shocked and surprised if I said God is not most obviously to be found at church services like this one, or at countless thousands of other church services taking place all over the world at this time, no matter how impressive their candlelit atmosphere, no matter how holy and special this night of all nights might be.

Instead, the very best chance of finding the God those two boys understand has gone missing is by looking – of all places – no further than right inside yourself.

Voice 2:

- When you look *inside* yourself, can you see the love that's there? Well, that's God, because by definition, God *is* Love.

- When you look inside yourself, do you see a generosity that knows it wants to give? That's God, because God *is* the Great and Generous Giver.

- And when you look inside yourself, do you recognise the presence of goodwill? That's God as well, or at least something of God, because God *is* Goodwill; God is 'Best Wishes'; God is the sincerity behind 'I hope you have a really happy Christmas, whoever you are.'

Voice 3:

Maybe you are one of those folk who comes to church every week. Or maybe you're one of those who hasn't been inside a church since this time last year. It doesn't make any difference. Anybody who chooses to stand outside themselves in order to look inside themselves will be able to catch at least glimpses of the not-missing-at-all, but wholly and totally present, living God.

Voice 4:

And that's what we celebrate together here tonight when we talk about the birth of God: 'Pleased as man with man to dwell'. Or, to translate those words into more appropriate language for today: 'God alive, with and within each one of his people; flesh of our flesh, bone of our bone, God come to earth'. Look inside yourself, and there you will see evidence of God present. Look at the people around you – any one of them – and you'll see the same thing there too. This is the Good News of Christmas. It is the distillation and essence of what this birth of God means and what it's all about. He came down to earth from heaven – so he could move and live and grow in you, and you in him.

Voice 1:

Fortunately those boys didn't ever get the punishment they expected for stealing God. How could they? It would have been absurd. For God never was missing in the first place. God was always there with and within them:

- even when they mischievously set fire to wheelie bins

- even when they rounded up unsuspecting cats

- even when, out of sheer devilment, they tied a couple of door handles together, and tormented an unfortunate old woman.

Voice 2:

As adults, whatever we get up to that we shouldn't, whatever we don't do that we should, God still point-blank refuses to give up his life and living in us. For Love has come, and Love is here, and Love is eternal and everlasting.

Voice 3:

So tonight, as on every other night:

God living in you.
God living in me.
Good reason to celebrate.

Voice 4:

Good reason then to tell all who will listen:

Christ is born!
God is indeed alive!
Christ the Redeemer is here!

THE MYSTERY OF THE INCARNATION

Holmes and Watson could be seated in armchairs facing each other, at the front, with the narrator speaking from the lectern. A few basic props as suggested by the text (a pipe, a large book wrapped in brown paper ...) will add to the atmosphere.

Narrator:

If you like the novels of Sir Arthur Conan Doyle, you will appreciate the Bible readings for today. They hold all the clues necessary to enable us to solve a very great mystery: the mystery of the Incarnation itself. But to solve this mystery, we need to employ the techniques of observation and imagination: qualities that were the trademark of the great detective himself – Sherlock Holmes.

On a day such as this, a knock came to the door of that famous house at 221B Baker Street, London. The good Dr Watson answered, but there was nobody there. On the mat, however, the anonymous caller had left a parcel wrapped in brown paper, and inside (unlikely as it might seem) is a copy of a book entitled the *Revised Common Lectionary*.

Predictably, Dr Watson is puzzled. He shows the book to Holmes, who is sitting by the fire in the parlour, smoking his pipe.

Holmes flicks through the pages pensively. To the uninitiated, the *Revised Common Lectionary* is as boring and uninteresting a read as a book of logarithm tables, or the endless lists of words in the *Crossword Lover's Companion*. But to the inquisitive mind of Sherlock Holmes, the *Revised Common Lectionary* holds a certain fascination. He knows that all the major Churches have been involved in producing page after page of selected Bible passages: readings appropriate to each Sunday of the Christian year, and that these lists have been designed to ensure that all the main themes of faith are covered over a period of time.

Sherlock Holmes:

How curious, Watson! How singularly curious ...

Narrator:

... he mumbles as he looks up the readings for today, the first Sunday after Christmas, which is when the church celebrates the Incarnation, the technical term for the birth of Jesus Christ. When Holmes scans the recommended passages, he is intrigued because neither the Old Testament reading from the Book of Samuel nor the New Testament reading from Luke's Gospel has anything to do with the sacred infant, all divine, born for us on earth below. There's not a single word about the birth of God's

Son at Christmas. So he reads them out loud to Watson, who by this time (perhaps like you) is ready to nod off to sleep.

Sherlock Holmes:

My dear Watson, will you just listen to this?

Readings: 1 Samuel 2:18–21, 26; Luke 2:41–52

Dr Watson:

It's obvious, my dear Holmes! Someone is deliberately trying to put us off the scent. These passages have nothing to do with the birth of the Christ child. It's a wild goose chase, a red herring. The answer to the mystery of the Incarnation lies elsewhere.

Sherlock Holmes:

Possibly, possibly ...

Narrator:

... murmurs Sherlock, and the clock can be heard ticking loudly as stillness settles on the room. But Holmes' mind is anything but still or settled as he reads these passages again to himself, and as his trained mind begins to pick out certain similarities and parallels between them.

Sherlock Holmes:

The scene and the setting: in both cases, the temple. The characters involved: two adolescent boys and their respective parents, especially their mothers – they feature large. The purpose of their visit: in each case the annual pilgrimage to make their sacrifice. Admittedly the young Samuel is already permanently resident in the old temple at Shiloh, working out his apprenticeship for the priesthood, as it were, whereas the boy Jesus, on the other hand, makes only a temporary visit to the new temple at Jerusalem.

Narrator:

But then the detective's eyes fall on something that makes him sit up sharply in his seat. In Samuel, he reads this:

Sherlock Holmes:

'The boy Samuel continued to grow and gain favour both with the Lord and with men.'

Narrator:

And then, this almost self-same sentence, supposedly written quite independently several hundred years later, but repeated virtually word for word in the New Testament by Luke.

Sherlock Holmes:

'Jesus grew both in body and in wisdom, gaining favour with God and men.'

Narrator:

Never one to accept such coincidences without question, Holmes smiles to himself as he feels the mystery beginning to unravel.

Sherlock Holmes:

Watson! Watson! Have you ever wondered about the integrity of this man Luke? Did it ever cross your mind that as he sat down to compose his own story, he had the Book of Samuel lying open in front of him? Has it ever occurred to you that he simply lifted some of the words from the Samuel story and inserted them into his own Jesus story? Is it too much to conjecture that, in places, Luke was no more than a plagiarist: a great big copycat?

Dr Watson:

So Holmes, do you deduce Luke copied bits of Samuel? Is that what you are suggesting? But if so, why, and for what purpose?

Sherlock Holmes:

My dear fellow, to understand that you need to try to put yourself in the place of Luke's audience, who were, of course, first-century Jews. Because they lived in an oral culture, they put great store in being able to recite chapter after chapter of their scriptures off by heart. In that way, their tradition was passed on by word of mouth. What's more, you have to appreciate that in those days, they knew their Jewish Bible (what we now refer to as the Old Testament) inside out. Therefore as soon as they heard these words about the boy Jesus from Luke, immediately they would recognise them as properly belonging to the story of Samuel who *'grew and gained favour both with the Lord and with men'*. Don't you see, Watson, that, by deliberately connecting Jesus with Samuel in this way, Luke was making a very important point about the humanity of Jesus.

Narrator:

Watson put a few more pieces of coal on the fire, re-lit his cigar and settled down comfortably to hear what else Holmes had to say. Holmes continued.

Sherlock Holmes:

The scene and the setting: in both cases, the temple: the place where ordinary humans go to meet their God. And Luke's Jesus, like any other human, goes to the temple to meet his God. Samuel is a young boy; a human boy: Luke's Jesus is a young boy; a human boy. Samuel is born of a human mother: Luke's Jesus is born of a human mother. The purpose of the family visits: in both cases, sacrifice, which is what humans do for their God.

Dr Watson:

So all the time, Luke talking about Jesus by pointing to Samuel. All the time, Luke aligning Jesus with Samuel, firmly placing Jesus beside Samuel, who is not a god. All the time, Luke stressing the humanity of Jesus by stressing the humanity of Samuel. And yet, all the time, Luke pointing to the divinity of Jesus precisely by setting him alongside Samuel, and thus inviting, compelling a comparison to be made between the two of them.

Sherlock Holmes:

But there is no comparison, Watson. For unlike Samuel, contained within Jesus' absolute humanity is also his absolute divinity. And this is the great mystery of the Incarnation: Jesus, born a human child, and yet a divine King.

Dr Watson:

Yes, yes, Holmes. I can see how Luke wants us to understand that Jesus is human like Samuel: like the rest of us; human in every way. But what I'm not clear about is what makes this human Jesus at one and the same time divine. It's the divine bit I find difficult.

Sherlock Holmes:

Watson, the human Jesus is divine because he is able to overcome his humanness. In his dealings with people, in his handling of all the issues of life, in confronting himself, he wrestles and struggles and strives and attains perfect goodness. Without exception, every single time he achieves it. This is what makes Godness. This is what it is to be divine.

Dr Watson:

But my dear Holmes, surely this is not unique to Jesus. I have seen some of this in other people: those who strive hard to care; those who struggle to do more than is expected of them; those who, having wrestled with themselves, come to the point of being able to forgive even the worst offences committed against them. Holmes, there are a number of instances where you can observe and identify this divinity in people.

Sherlock Holmes:

That's true, Watson. The line between humanity and divinity is sometimes quite thin. One of the psalm writers makes that very point when he says: *'What are mere human beings that you care for them so much? Yet you have made humanity only a little inferior than gods, and have crowned us with glory and honour.'*

Notice carefully, Watson: only a *little* inferior. And that is exactly what Luke is trying to say by putting the boy Jesus right next to the boy Samuel. The line between humanity and divinity is sometimes very thin. But that line is there, and the distinction remains and always will. But what makes Jesus divine is that he crosses the line.

Look at his consistency in attaining the ideal, his comprehensiveness in achieving complete and total victory over himself every time, his ability to overcome the inherent limitations and restrictions of his humanity. That is what makes Jesus God, and that is what makes the human Jesus of Bethlehem the divine Christ of Calvary.

Dr Watson:

Well done, old chap! You've done it again! The mystery of the Incarnation is solved.

Sherlock Holmes:

Elementary, my dear Watson, elementary! But only as far as it goes. For what remains is equally mysterious. If the line that exists is so thin, if divinity is sometimes within your grasp and mine, then what debars us, what restricts us, what prevents us from struggling and wrestling for such goodness ourselves, in the same way that Jesus did?

Dr Watson:

Holmes, I'm surprised at you! I'm surprised you can't see it. Because that too is elementary. There is nothing! There is absolutely nothing at all!

DIY CHRISTMAS WORSHIP

Ask different people to lead the different sections of this service, which (apart from the first and final hymns and the dismissal and blessing) may happen in any order, as folk think appropriate. The worship leader may wish to introduce the service and announce the first and final hymns.

Hymns

Opening hymn: 'Joy to the world' (CH4 320)
'It was on a starry night' (CH4 302)
'See him lying on a bed of straw' (CH4 310)
'Jesus is born' (CH4 311)
'Who would think' (CH4 295)
Closing hymn: 'Angels from the realms of glory' (CH4 324)

Reading: John: 1:1–18 (from *The Message*)

The Word was first,
the Word present to God,
God present to the Word.
The Word was God,
in readiness for God from day one.
Everything was created through him;
nothing – not one thing! –
came into being without him.
What came into existence was Life,
and the Life was Light to live by.
The Life-Light blazed out of the darkness;
the darkness couldn't put it out.

There once was a man, his name John, sent by God to point out the way to the Life-Light. He came to show everyone where to look, who to believe in. John was not himself the Light; he was there to show the way to the Light.

The Life-Light was the real thing:
Every person entering Life
he brings into Light.
He was in the world,

the world was there through him,
and yet the world didn't even notice.
He came to his own people,
but they didn't want him.
But whoever did want him,
who believed he was who he claimed
and would do what he said,
He made to be their true selves,
their child-of-God selves.
These are the God-begotten,
not blood-begotten,
not flesh-begotten,
not sex-begotten.

The Word became flesh and blood,
and moved into the neighborhood.
We saw the glory with our own eyes,
the one-of-a-kind glory,
like Father, like Son,
Generous inside and out,
true from start to finish.

John pointed him out and called, 'This is the One! The One I told
you was coming after me but in fact was ahead of me. He has
always been ahead of me, has always had the first word.'

We all live off his generous bounty,
gift after gift after gift.
We got the basics from Moses,
and then this exuberant giving and receiving,
This endless knowing and understanding –
all this came through Jesus, the Messiah.
No one has ever seen God,
not so much as a glimpse.
This one-of-a-kind God-Expression,
who exists at the very heart of the Father,
has made him plain as day.*

Lighting the Christ candle on the Advent wreath

Every week throughout Advent, candles are lit in churches. They are a sign of the light of God coming into this world, bringing hope and peace and love and joy. Throughout Advent, the candle flames burn with expectation, and reflect the anticipation of the people of God, who wait for the birth of Light and Life. But now, unto us a child is born; unto us a son is given. And so today we light the Christ candle. It tells us that Love came down at Christmas, and that Love has come to stay.

Light the Christ candle

Christmas quiz

We've heard the Christmas story so many times. But how much of it is true, and how much of it is tradition? Here's a wee quiz to help us sort things out.

1. How many wise men were there?

a) Three
b) Two
c) Four
d) We don't know

(Nobody knows. The Bible mentions three gifts, but doesn't say how many wise men brought them.)

2. Who were the wise men anyway? What was their job?

a) Eastern kings
b) Magicians
c) Academics
d) Astrologers

(They were men who studied the natural sciences, including the stars.)

3. How did Mary get to Bethlehem?

a) She and Joseph walked
b) Riding on a donkey
c) Nobody knows

(The Bible doesn't say how they got there. There's no mention of a donkey.)

4. What is a 'heavenly host'?

a) A choir of angels
b) A group of saints
c) An army
d) Nobody knows

(Elsewhere in the Bible, the words 'heavenly host' refer to an army.)

5. How many angels spoke to the shepherds?

a) A multitude
b) Two
c) Nobody knows

(Only one angel spoke. According to Luke 2:10: The angel said to them, 'Don't be afraid …')

6. What song did the angels sing?

a) Joy to the world
b) Hark! The herald angels sing
c) Glory to God in the highest
d) None of these

(None of these, not even C. They sang 'Glory to God in highest heaven'.)

7. When did the baby Jesus cry?

a) When he opened the presents from the wise men
b) When he was hungry
c) When he needed his nappy changed
d) When the cattle started lowing
e) He didn't cry at all ('the little Lord Jesus, no crying he makes')

(We don't know. But he was a human baby and was bound to cry sometime.)

8. What did the innkeeper say to Mary and Joseph?

a) 'Come in, you're very welcome.'
b) 'I can give you the honeymoon suite.'
c) 'The inn is full, but there's a stable out the back.'
d) 'There's no room at the inn.'

(There's no mention of an innkeeper in the Gospel accounts.)

9. Where was Jesus born?

a) In a stable
b) In an inn
c) In a house
d) In a cave

(We don't know. The Bible doesn't say where he was born. All it says is he was laid in a manger.)

10. When Mary was told she was going to have a baby, were she and Joseph

a) Just good friends?
b) Recently married?
c) Engaged to be married?

(They were engaged to be married.)

11. Which animals were there when the baby was born?

a) donkeys
b) cows
c) sheep
d) goats
e) mice

(The Bible doesn't mention any animals at all.)

12. When the wise men brought their gifts to Jesus, where did they find him?

a) In a house
b) In a stable
c) In a manger
d) None of these

(In a house)

Prayer

Child in the manger, infant of Mary,
you have come and made our home your home.
So no more far away, but here and now,
with us and within us;
listening, healing, mending,
teaching, suffering and forgiving.
A fragile child in a frightening world,
while shepherds listen and wonder.
An innocent child in a hostile world,
and wise men bring their presents.
A rejected child in a dangerous world
where only some want to kneel
and some give you the gift of themselves.

But we will welcome you warmly,
and cuddle you snugly and keep you safe.
We will hold you dearly
when we see you; when we hear you;
when we find you in our midst:
in the tears of the grieving ones;
in the laughter of the delighted ones;
in the silence of the fearful ones;
in the pain of those who need your company;
in the pain which belongs to ourselves.

And so we feel for you now,
in the secret and personal parts of our lives
that only we know and you know:
in our thinking and dreaming and hoping;
in our regrets and aspirations,
and in our best imaginings too.

Immanuel: God-with-us,
patiently waiting to be acknowledged;
desperate to share with us your peace.

Time of quiet

Thanks be to God.
His light is in the world:
the light that never dies;
the meaning that gives our being
all purpose and reason.
Amen

A Christmas story

It was two days before Christmas and Nicholas and Hannah were very excited. They were walking home from school in the snow. They'd had their Christmas service that after-noon, and had heard the Christmas story – all about wise men, and shepherds and angels in the sky, and the baby Jesus born under a star and laid in a manger. At the end of the story, the teacher had said that on Christmas Eve, the Christ child visits those who wait and watch for him coming.

Hannah, who always thought deep thoughts, said to Nicholas: 'What if Jesus comes to us? Maybe we should have a gift for him. After all, it's his birthday. But what could we give him?' Nicholas was the practical one:

'Getting Jesus a present would be OK, but how will we be able to recognise him? We don't know what kind of present we should get. We don't even know what he looks like.'

'You're right,' said Hannah. 'We don't know what Jesus looks like. But I think we should get a present all the same. Three presents – just to be on the safe side. We'll ask mum what we should get. She'll be sure to know.'

When they got home, that was the first thing Hannah asked. 'Mum, what kind of gift does a baby need?' 'Well, when a baby feels warm, it knows it's loved,' said Mum. 'So, I suppose a blanket would be a good idea.'

Nicholas asked his dad. 'Dad, what would be a good thing to give a baby?' 'Well, it is always good for people to see where they're going in life, so I think a torch might be a very useful gift.'

That was two out of the three presents taken care of. What could be the third gift? 'I've got it,' said Hannah. 'How about the selection box Auntie Margaret gave us to share? That would be a good gift. Even if a baby can't chew, it can suck on the chocolate.' Nicholas agreed.

Hannah and Nicholas stayed up late that night. They sewed a blanket together using extra pieces of fabric from their mum's sewing box. 'There, that's really pretty,' Hannah said. 'And it's warm! If Jesus comes as a baby, he'll know he's loved.'

The next morning they set their minds to procuring a torch. Nicholas had seen torches that didn't need batteries – the kind you wind up – in a shop in the High Street. So they emptied their piggy banks and set off into town to buy one. It was really busy on a Saturday morning and Mr Anderson, the shopkeeper, looked run off his feet.

'What can I do for you two this fine cold morning?' he asked. 'We want to buy one of those wind-up torches – the ones that never need batteries.' 'Good choice, that's one of my best sellers. They're five pounds.' 'Oh,' said Hannah, disappointed. 'We only have three pounds between us. Are there any torches for three pounds?'

Mr Anderson looked at them and said: 'I have an idea. I need two strong people to carry these empty boxes to the tip at the end of the road. They're getting in the way of the customers. If you could work for me this morning, I could pay you each a pound and you could buy the torch.' It was hard work, but when they were done, they had a shiny silver wind-up torch.

That afternoon, the doorbell rang. It was their next-door neighbour Mrs Wood. She said: 'It's our central heating boiler. It's packed in, and the house is freezing. We wondered if you had an electric fire you could lend us.' 'Of course, that's no problem,' said Dad, and he went out to the garage to find the fire.

Nicholas overheard this conversation, and ran to find Hannah. 'The Wood's heating has broken down, and they have a new baby.' Hannah knew what he was thinking: Babies who are warm know they're loved. So the pair of them got the blanket they had made and took it over to the Wood's house.

That night it was Christmas Eve, and the family were going to the late-night service in the church. Nicholas and Hannah decided to bring the two presents they had left (the torch and the selection box), just in case Jesus was in church.

As they got near to the church, they noticed a man standing beside his car. The bonnet was up and he was looking into the engine. Dad went over to see if he could help. 'The electrics have failed,' said the man. 'But I've phoned my brother-in-law and he's coming to see if he can fix it.' 'All the same,' said Dad, 'you need to be able to see in the dark.' Hannah and Nicholas looked at each other and they held out the new torch and said 'Merry Christmas'. The man was very, very grateful.

When they arrived at the church, Hannah and Nicholas overheard a conversation between some of the adults. 'What a shame,' somebody was saying. 'Did you hear that the Wilson family were burgled and all the presents have been stolen from under the tree?'

Sam Wilson was the same age as Nicholas. In fact, they were in the same class at school, and were good pals. Nicholas looked at Hannah and she smiled. From inside his jacket pocket Nicholas pulled out the selection box – the third and last gift they had wanted to give to the baby Jesus. Nicholas walked down the aisle to where Sam and his family were sitting. 'Hi Sam,' he said. 'I'm sorry to hear things were stolen from your house. This is for you.' He gave Sam the selection box.

After church, Nicholas and Hannah were speaking to Mr Allan, the minister. They told him about the presents they had for Jesus, and what had happened, and that now they didn't have anything to give to the newborn baby. But Mr Allan told them about one of the most important things Jesus ever said, when he was a grown man.

One day Jesus told his friends that whenever they gave to people who were in need, then it was the same as giving him a gift. 'I don't think you should worry,' said Mr Allan. 'I think you have already given Jesus your gifts. I hope you have a lovely day tomorrow. Happy Christmas!'

Sally Foster-Fulton

The offering

Dismissal and blessing

When the star in the sky disappears,
when the shepherds go back to their hillside,
when the wise men return to wherever they came from,
then the real work of Christmas begins.

God bless us, and keep us safe
on this day, on all days,
in all the time to come.
God blesses us, each and every one.

* Scripture quotations from The Message. *Copyright © by Eugene H. Peterson 1993, 1994, 1995, 1996, 2000, 2001, 2002. Used by permission of NavPress Publishing Group.*

MYSTERY GOD

Voice 1:

Mystery God,
we will never know all about you:
who and what you are,
how and why you exist,
all the ways and means that you are Love.
Such is your greatness
that we can only catch glimpses of you,
and understand parts of you.

Because we are not gods, but human,
in our limitation we find it impossible to know all of you.

Voice 2:

But we do know you treasure us as your own,
because we are your very own,
made and meant by you.
And we know too
that you long for us to be free of ourselves:
transformed people; changed people.

Voice 1:

You even came yourself to show us how.

Voice 2:

Joy of heaven, and now to earth come down,
empower us to go even beyond the second mile
in our caring.

Voice 1:

Child of Bethlehem, Love divine,
show us how to struggle with ourselves,
so that we are prepared to strive
to give even more of who we are.

Voice 2:

Man of Calvary, All-Compassion,
because of your forgiveness
we can learn how to forgive each other.
We can even learn how to forgive ourselves.

Voice 1:

And so, this mysterious birth of yours
bringing salvation and new life,
so that we and all your world become a new creation,
and your kingdom becomes established here on earth.

Voice 2:

So will you encourage us to strive for something of your divinity:
to be conscious of our potential in this new year?
And as we turn the corner of new and exciting tomorrows,
help us to embrace your future gladly,
and welcome all it offers with a spirit of hope.

Epiphany

WHERE ARE THE ANGELS?

Readings: Jeremiah 31:15; Matthew 2:13–18

Voice 1:

He was a beautiful baby: eyes dark as night that could light up a room when he was happy; soft, chubby baby-skin that smelled so good and felt so warm against your cheek. He'd already mastered the petted lip, and could melt your heart – and your resolve – with one soulful look.

He'd just started making determined noises: cooing and gurgling really – but his older brother and sister insisted they knew exactly what he wanted, and his father swore he was trying to say 'Daddy'. The time for walking was just around the corner, and already the breakable things were getting put up. The baby-proof shelves and boxes were fuller than before. He loved to pull himself up, and they'd all take turns holding him in their laps and letting him scramble up, using their hair as a ladder, waiting for that incredible baby laugh that seemed to come from his toes.

He was their beautiful boy. At the end of the day he was sung to sleep with that song. Maybe you've heard it:

All night, all day, angels watching over me, my Lord.
All night, all day, angels watching over me.

And they'd pray that an angel would watch him as he slept: their baby; their beautiful wee boy.

They believed in God. They couldn't *not* believe, after having been given such beautiful gifts in their children. But they had to ask and be angry sometimes at this God they believed in. Where was their angel that night when the men came and took the little one away? 'Orders,' the men had said. 'Collateral damage', they'd called him. Their beautiful baby, their lovely wee boy. *What about him?* they couldn't help but wonder, when they heard the rumours of the one who'd escaped. They couldn't help but wonder, if God went to so much trouble to warn one family, why there weren't enough angels to go round? Where was their angel then? Only heaven knows.

Solo: 'Angels watching over me'

Voice 2:

They were such beautiful babies, all of them, in war-torn places, in the villages and towns ripped apart by violence and hatred all over the world. Yet Herods continue to issue their orders and cause untold 'collateral damage'. All over the world mothers and fathers, their eyes dark with grief, ask the same question: 'Why? Why my beautiful baby?' But still it doesn't melt cold hearts or resolve.

At the end of the day, what songs do we have to sing them to sleep? 'All night, all day, angels watching over me, my Lord. All night, all day, angels watching over me.' Can we still pray that prayer in a world like ours? I believe in God. I couldn't *not* believe, after having been given such beautiful gifts in my own children. But I have to ask and be angry sometimes at this God I believe in. Where are these angels when the men come and take the children away? 'Orders,' they say. 'Collateral damage' they're called. These beautiful babies, these beloved children, what about them? I couldn't help but wonder about them when I read this story again about the one who'd escaped. I couldn't help but wonder, if God went to so much trouble to warn one family, why there weren't enough angels to go round. Where are those angels then? Only heaven knows.

Solo: 'Angels watching over me'

Voice 3:

I don't know about angels, but I do know a bit about good and evil, and I do believe that if God sends angels, then they probably look an awful lot like you and me. We don't always know what effect our actions are going to have, even our smallest actions. But if we act in faith, then what we do in faith may reach further than we could ever imagine.

In the film *The Lord of the Rings*, one of the main characters, Frodo Baggins, is feeling overwhelmed by what he has been asked to do: he has to destroy the ring that holds the power of all evil. He says that he wishes that none of this had come to him, and that he was home and everything had been as it was. But Gandalf, the wise wizard, reminds him that we don't have the ability to choose the time in which we live or the power to control what happens to us. We can only decide what we will do with the time given. That is within our power. If we choose to act in faith, then our actions may do more good than we'll ever know, or could ever possibly imagine.

If there are to be angels winging their way to the broken world we live in, then we must begin to fly. God's trust has been put in us. What will you choose to do with it?

They are such beautiful babies, in the refugee camps and the orphanages all over the world. Yet Herods continue to issue their orders and cause untold 'collateral damage'. All over the world, mothers and fathers, their eyes dark with grief, ask the same question: 'Why? Why my beautiful baby?'

If there are to be angels winging their way to the broken world, then we must begin to fly, work to melt cold hearts in order to weaken the resolve for war, act in faith, trusting that God will multiply our efforts. We need to hear the prayer: 'All night, all day, angels watching over me, my Lord. All night, all day, angels watching over me.' We need to be that prayer in this world of ours.

I can't help but wonder, when I read this story again about the one who escaped. I can't help but wonder, if God went to so much trouble to warn one family, why there still aren't enough angels to go round. Where are those angels? Only heaven knows. But maybe we do too.

Sally Foster-Fulton

LENT

THE TEMPTATIONS

This is intended to be used as part of small group worship. Provide each person with a copy of the 'A time for reflection' questions, and ask them to find personal space for reflection.

Reading: Luke 4:1–13

Comment

The first temptation is personal, and it is no accident it comes first, because seeing to ourselves first is possibly the biggest temptation we face. Turning stones into bread is about feeding ourselves: seeing our own needs as the priority; caring principally for our own well-being and contentment. The first temptation is about making sure our own wants and desires are met – the rest can take care of themselves.

The second temptation is political. 'I'll give you all this power and all this wealth,' the Devil says. The supremacy, hold or advantage that one human being can have over another by virtue of position or influence or resources or knowledge can be of stagger-ing proportion. This temptation is about how we conduct our relationships: whether or not we take advantage of those we know are weaker than us; whether we sometimes – or often – manipulate those we have the power to manipulate. The daily opportunities we have for all of this are endless.

The third temptation is religious. It is about making God or religion into our own personal pet; turning God into what we would wish him to be so that he becomes *my* personal protector, *my* guarantor of success. 'God is on my side, and not on yours.' This applies not only to individuals, but to nations who go to war adopting the moral high ground: they are on the side of right.

We take time now to reflect on these three types of temptations, and how (perhaps without even being aware of it) we may succumb to them.

A time for reflection

The Devil said: 'If you are God's Son, order this stone to turn into bread.' This tempta-tion is about looking to your own needs first.

- In what ways do you put yourself first?
- What methods do you use to ensure you are always protected and secure?
- Does being preoccupied with your own well-being mean that others receive less care from you than they should?

The Devil said: 'I will give you all this power and all this wealth. It has been handed over to me and I can give it to anyone I choose.' This temptation is about how we conduct our relationships.

- Do you sometimes take advantage of people by means of your knowledge, strength of character, resources, etc?
- What is your usual method for getting your own way?
- Do you control anyone in any way?

The Devil said: 'If you are God's Son, throw yourself down from here. For the scripture says: "God will order his angels to take good care of you. They will hold you up with their hands so that not even your feet will be hurt on the stones".' This temptation is about domesticating God.

- Do you expect God to do what you want (e.g. when you pray for someone who is ill to get better)?
- What do you do that must disappoint God?
- Is your idea of who and what God is too small?

THE DEVIL'S ~~TAIL~~ TALE

Devil (to congregation):

That damned Jesus! I'd tried before to get him. Umpteen times I'd tried, but it's never worked. But then a wonderful opportunity presented itself: a golden opportunity not to be missed. For some daft reason of his own, he took it into his head to roam around in the desert. *Right*, I thought. *Here's my chance. This should be a piece of cake! We'll see just how strong he is now!*

You have to appreciate I'm talking *desert* here – a hostile hellhole of heat. I mean, it was just cooking. And then at night time, the opposite. As soon as the sun goes down, the temperature plummets like a rocket. With nowhere to shelter, you just sit there and shiver through the long, dark hours. Hot and cold torture: that's enough to wear anybody down and break their resistance. But add to this the fact that he's had nothing to eat for 40 days, and you've got him at his most vulnerable: starving, filthy, weary, disorientated – susceptible. Here's my chance. Here's my chance to get him, and get him good.

Devil (to Jesus):

Eh, Jesus, are you feeling hungry by any chance?

Jesus:

I'm famished. I'm ravenous. My stomach thinks my throat's been cut.

Devil:

Well now, Jesus, you're the Son of God. You don't need to feel hungry at all. Why don't you do the sensible thing, and magic this boulder so it turns into bread?

Devil (to congregation):

Any normal person would have jumped at that possibility. Any other human, who was not a complete idiot, would have been unable to resist. You see, in circumstances like this, natural instinct kicks in; self-preservation takes over. But even in less urgent situations, the human compulsion is to satisfy personal desire.

I've lured countless numbers of people into my trap by pointing this out to them. And it was easy. 'You don't need to deny yourself at all!' I've said it many a time. 'Grab whatever you want: food, money, sex, the bigger share. Fill your pockets. Charity begins at home. Take whatever you want and take it for yourself.' And they have. It usually works like a dream every time.

Jesus (to congregation):

But self-gratification through having and procuring and possessing is not the only thing that keeps people alive. You can have every material object you could ever possibly long for, and still not be fulfilled or feel complete. Women and men have other needs; deeper needs. The need of the human soul must also be met. And that's why people have always searched for their God.

Since the beginning of time, there has always been a gnawing, a yearning, a persistent seeking for some power outwith and beyond humanity. For spirit and soul are restless. They also get hungry and have to be fed. And the only one who can meet that essential, basic human need is the God of heaven himself.

Jesus (to Devil):

You are good at your work of persuading. And so you should be: you are long-practised at it and have had great successes. But men and women cannot live on bread alone.

God, have mercy on me and keep me strong. God, have mercy on me and help me to resist. God, have mercy on me …

Chant: 'Kyrie eleison' (from *Many and Great*, or *Come All You People*)

Devil (to congregation):

He's such a smartie, isn't he? Such a goody two-shoes! But at the same time, he is such a fool. I was trying to get him to take care of himself, and feed his pressing physical desires. Yet he tells me the bigger priority is to tend to the health of his soul.

Devil (to Jesus):

Jesus, I want you to come on a little trip with me. I want to take you out of this horrible desert and give you a bit of a break.

Come with me, and the pair of us will go on a wee jaunt to Jerusalem. We'll go on my magic carpet, and it will take us up to the very highest pinnacle of the temple ...

Jesus, I hope you've got a good head for heights. This is a really dangerous place to be. There's a 450-foot drop here, and you could end up at the bottom of the Kedron Valley. So you need to hold on, and be very careful where you put your feet. But come to think of it, that doesn't actually apply in your case, does it? In fact, it's really quite academic. For if you did happen to fall, or even if you decided to jump, God would order his angels to rush in and catch you. They'd rescue you before your feet could touch the ground.

Come on, Jesus. Injury is impossible for you; even self-inflicted injury. If he loves you like you say, then you don't need to worry. Go for it! Jump! You know you've got nothing to lose.

Jesus (to Devil):

You think you're quite clever, don't you? But I see through your game. This time it's not about my own self-gratification. What you're asking me to do is make God my own little pampered pet. You want me to turn God into what *I* want him to be, so that he becomes *my* personal protector; *my* minder; *my* insurance policy. You want me to ask him to be *my* guarantor of success.

Jesus (to congregation):

That's how a lot of people understand God. They want to use him

for their own benefit. They think they can tame God so that he fits conveniently into their own agenda. And so:

- Holy wars are fought in the name of God: 'Right is on our side, and God will make sure that we win.' Moral high ground is established; and arguments are started because each opponent is certain it is they, and not their enemy, who know what God's mind is.
- Some pray for rain, while next door, others are flooded out.
- Some pray for their own success, and expect God to secure it for them – as if he should respond to only *their* cries, and block his ears to the pleadings of others who are also desperate for success.

Jesus (to Devil):

Mr Devil, you are good at your work of persuading. And it's true you have had many great successes. But I will not try to own God. I will not put the Lord my God to the test.

God, have mercy on me and keep me strong. God, have mercy on me in this hard struggle to resist. God, have mercy on me …

Chant: 'Kyrie eleison'

Devil (to congregation):

I'm not sure what to make of this guy. He's tougher than I thought, and I think he can see through my ploys of persuasion. I need to dream up an offer he just can't refuse. I have to present him with something really tantalising; something quite irresistible this time round.

Devil (to Jesus):

Jesus, we'll go on another mind-trip, you and I. This time, to the top of a very high mountain, so you'll be able to survey all this world's kingdoms, and see how glorious they are … You can have them. They're yours – every single one, lock, stock and barrel. Jesus, think of the kudos when your name's up there in bright lights. Think of the influence you'll be able to exert. Think of the power and the wealth, and all the accolades you'll receive. And all you need to do for this to happen is to pledge your allegiance to me.

Jesus (to Devil):

Get away from me! Leave me alone! You are dangling a carrot before me that's rotten through and through. You want me to put myself in a position of absolute power so that I'll have absolute supremacy. I know you've done it many times before, and it has worked, for what you are suggesting is, admittedly, very attractive.

Jesus (to congregation):

For people in power can manipulate those weaker than themselves. They can exploit their status, and who and what they are for their own advantage and gain.

It happens all the time when people have been convinced by the silver-tongued cajoling of this evil fox:

- It happens in families, where the strong threaten the weak with physical abuse.
- It happens in workplaces, where rank is misused, and lower rank is abused.
- It happens between nations, where wealth and possessions, and superiority and sophistication result in an obscene exploitation of the weak and the hungry and the poor.
- And it even happens in churches, where knowledge is power; strength of character is power; abilities and skills are used for power.

Jesus (to Devil):

You are good at your work of persuading, and it is true you have had many successes. But I will not worship at your throne of enticement. I will not sell my soul to you. I will be true to God alone, and will serve only him.

God, have mercy on me and keep me strong. God, have mercy on me in this difficult struggle. God, have mercy on me …

Chant: 'Kyrie eleison'

Devil (to congregation):

You can't say I didn't try. I used all my best arguments, but I'll admit it: I have met my match in him. Others were easy meat, but he's a tough nut to crack, this Jesus.

And so I left him, this damned Jesus, fool that he is. I left him in all his torment and all his distress in that hostile desert.

Let him stew there for now, because there will be other chances, and I'm not giving up. So I'll bide my time, and I'll watch, and I'll wait, and then I'll try again.

But in the meantime, there are always his supporters to have a go at: the ones who think they're perfectly safe because they've decided to follow him. What they don't realise is that they could work up the same resolve to resist me as he did. But to be able to do that, they'd have to get down on their knees, and ask for the help of the one they choose to call the Spirit of the living God.

Song: 'I bow my knee in prayer' (CG 56)

THE TREE

For this reflection you will need last year's dried-out Christmas tree.

Voice 1:

Followers of Jesus, we have come to a turning point in our journey. Once we followed a star. Now we wander in the wilderness. Once we heard angel voices, and the wise spoke in hushed, awed tones before a baby. Now the voices have begun to harden and the angry tones sometimes hide fear.

We come back bringing a symbol of the birth of our Saviour. This is the Christmas tree which stood here in December: a sign of hope and promise and new beginning, decorated with children's creations and elegant trimmings and treasures stored up through the years. Beautiful and fragrant and alive it was, but look at it now. It is a sign of death and decay and ageing. Stripped of branches and shoots and potential it stands barren and desolate and forlorn. Look at it now. Of what use is it to us, this broken symbol of life? What will we do with it now? What good word could it possibly speak to us now? How will it resurrect itself for us?

Voice 2:

We could make it into a crutch: a symbol of healing and restoring and helping. Jesus cured the sick and the lame. He showed compassion for the hurting ones. Remember the paralysed man, the woman with the bleeding, the blind and the deaf, the dead child? We could make it into a crutch.

Jesus:

I said to the paralysed man, take up your mat and go home. I told the little girl to get up, but I told those around her to give her something to eat. The power to heal came from me, but the woman who touched my cloak had faith and desperately desired to be whole again. There are many who are not healed physically, but there is wholeness. I am a healer and an enabler, but do not make a crutch of me.

Voice 3:

We could make it into a stick: a weapon to be used, but only on the backs of oppressors of course ... and on those who disagree, or disobey, or are disgruntled. After all, Jesus got angry. He yelled at the scribes and the Pharisees. He got exasperated with his own disciples. He tore the temple apart in a fit of temper. We could make it into a stick – a weapon.

Jesus:

Of course I got angry and exasperated, and I did lose control when I saw how God's house was being misused. My righteous anger should be an example to my Body. But I also said: 'Blessed are the peacemakers, and the meek.' I said: 'Turn the other cheek. Leave the judging to God. Forgive always.' I am angry and exasperated when my children are hurt, but my angry voice cries out for peace. I am not a weapon.

Voice 4:

We could make it into a kind of building: a monument to God and a memorial to Jesus, like the booths the disciples never got to build, like the temple Solomon erected, like the buildings we have now with solid walls to protect us and hard seats to keep us in a straight line. We could make it into a kind of building.

Jesus:

The Son of Man has no place to lay his head, and I am not to be found contained within walls – even sanctuary walls. I am a Spirit, infinite and eternal. Do not confine me to a building.

Voice 5:

We could leave it just as it is and not change a thing. As long as it lasts, we can close our eyes and remember Christmas: gifts and lights and baubles and happy times. Jesus is all about love and innocence and the peace of Christmas morning. We could leave it as it is and not change a thing.

Jesus:

Forget the former things. Remember them not. Behold! I am about to do a new thing. I am the Way, the Truth and the Life, and life is always moving, and change does not equal decay. The Spirit breathes newness. It blows and changes and stirs. I am about love and innocence and peace, but I am also a warner, a teacher, an inspirer. The peace I offer is not always an easy one, but one to be fought for. And when the Spirit blows, nothing is left as it was.

Voice 6:

We could just burn it. At least it would do some good. What use is it just sitting here? If we burn it, it will give heat. We could warm ourselves, and others, with it. Jesus was a doer. He wouldn't have wanted it to be wasted. We could just burn it.

Jesus:

When I was at dinner once with friends, a woman came and poured oil of tremendous cost on my feet, wiping them with her hair, mixing the oil with her tears. There was something eternal in her gesture.

There was a symbol and a message in it. Some grumbled and called her a waster, but I did not agree. I was not to be with them forever, but the story of her love lives for ever in the remembering of her gesture. It has not been wasted.

Voice 1:

So what will we do with this tree, once a sign of hope and promise and new beginning, decorated with children's creations and elegant trimmings and treasures stored up through the years, beautiful and fragrant and alive? Look at it now: a sign of death and decay and ageing; stripped of branches and shoots and potential; barren and desolate and forlorn. Look at it now. Of what use is it to us, this broken symbol of life; this symbol of broken life? What will we do with it now? What good word could it possibly speak to us now? How will it resurrect itself?

(Someone comes and ties the tree into the shape of a cross.)

Jesus:

In the cross, I turned a sign of death and decay and betrayal into a sign of eternal hope and promise and new beginning. In the face of hatred and ugliness, this cross, once desolate and barren and forlorn, stands for love that turned the world on its head; love that brings wholeness and healing; love that speaks strongly for peace; love that cannot be contained in any building (not even a sanctuary!); and love that never stops, but blows with a spirit of newness, leaving nothing untouched.

I was not to be with you forever, but this story of love lives for ever in the remembering and living of it. And that is how I will resurrect.

Sally Foster-Fulton

HOLY WEEK

THE BRIEFEST OF ENCOUNTERS

Palm Sunday in Jerusalem.
The shouting gets louder,
the noise swells to a roar.
'Hosanna!' is the cry of the crowd.
'Blessings on him who comes in the name of the Lord!'

You are there that day;
one of that great throng of people
tightly packed together in the streets,
waiting for Jesus to come.

Can you hear their cheering?
Look at all the colour.
Inside you feel excited and expectant
just like the rest of them.

(Pause)

O my God!
Here he comes now:
Jesus the Messiah;
Jesus, his people's Redeemer;
Jesus, the Saviour of the world.

You join in the cheering as well.
Caught up in the excitement of the moment,
you also shout 'Hosanna!
Blessings on him who comes in the name of the Lord!'

(Pause)

As Jesus passes,
riding on the back of a donkey,
he is smiling.
For one brief moment,
among all the people in that crowd,
he catches your eye.
No words are exchanged,
but his look says everything

because, clearly, he understands how you feel.
And under your breath
there are a few words you keep on repeating.
Over and over again, you whisper them silently.
Over and over again, some words that you want him to know.

Say them to him now, as your eyes meet his.
Say them to him now, as his eyes meet yours.

Time of quiet

Jesus has not heard your words.
How could he?
The noise is too great;
the people are too many;
the moment of meeting too short.

But he has understood you all right,
for the smile on his face breaks even wider
and the depth of his love for you shines from his eyes.

And then he looks away.
The donkey carries him on.
Others like you will shout their praises.

'Hosanna! Hosanna! Hosanna!
Blessings on him who comes in the name of the Lord!'

MARY ANOINTS JESUS

Before the service, fill a little dish with fragrant oil (for example, lavender oil). At the close of the service, people come forward to have the sign of the cross placed on their palm, as every-one sings 'Brother, sister, let me serve you' (CH4 694).

Reading: John 12:1–11

Comment

Mary pours this very expensive perfume over Jesus' feet. It was a dramatic gesture: a symbolic action on her part. It demonstrated the depth of her feeling and the extent of her love for him. It was also a recognition of his divinity and kingship.

But there's another aspect of this action of hers. Jesus had previously been doing a lot of walking on rocky, dusty roads. In all probability his feet were dry and cracked and sore. Maybe they were even covered with thickened skin and calluses. It was also a very practical thing that she did. It was basic, physical caring to meet his immediate need. The oil soothes his discomfort. She wants to take away his aches and his pains.

We don't often think of Jesus having homely little problems like sore feet, or a toothache, or an ingrown toenail, or a skelf in his finger. A sore heart and a troubled mind, certainly, but sore feet and things like that? They're never mentioned. But of course he did and he must have. Jesus was human after all.

So Mary pours out the expensive oil of kindness, and in all probability she could hardly afford it. But then those who criticised this extravagance overlooked, or wanted to ignore, that he had needs as well; that he also was poor and possessed nothing but what he stood up in that day. Her giving: they couldn't see the beauty in it, or the self-sacrifice, or the sacredness of her action. Nor could they perceive graciousness in his receiving, or humility in his acceptance of what she did.

None of us here is dirt-poor, but we each have needs; personal needs. And we know of other people who have needs as well. So I'd like to invite you to think about one person you know: perhaps someone in your family, or in the congregation, or at work. It could be a friend, or even someone you don't know quite so well. This person might have a specific physical need; or be alone and lonely and in need of company; or be hurting because they are not understood; or be someone who is feeling tentative about themselves, and who needs encouragement and affirmation.

Think of that one person, and then in the stillness here, promise to God that over the next week or two you will try to give them something of what it is they need. It could be your time or your company. It could be your encouragement or your support or your caring. It could be your words or your listening. It could be your patience and understanding, or rebuke.

And then, at the end of the time of reflection, as we sing our song, as a sign of your intention to carry through your promise, will you come forward, and hold out the palm of your hand, and allow me to place a little oil on it in the shape of a cross? The perfume will linger on your hand: a reminder of the promise you have made.

But before we do this, I should add a health warning:

It may involve you in costly generosity – such as Mary's generosity – to care meaningfully, significantly for the person you have been thinking about here today.

And it may take great humility on your part – such as the humility that Jesus had – to receive and accept and carry out the prompting of the Spirit of the love of God that comes to you through your thoughts in the silence.

A time of reflection

Song and action

WRITING YOUR OWN OBITUARY

Give each person a piece of paper and a pen before the service begins.

Death is in the air for Jesus, and he knows it full well.

- People have been listening to him, and the priests and holy people don't like it.
- He's gathered crowds round about him, and the Romans are twitchy and nervous.
- Now there are Gentiles, and even Greeks, seeking him out, convinced by his subversive, corrupting nonsense. It *can't* be allowed to continue. Something will have to be done.

Death is in the air for Jesus, and he knows it full well. Any reasonable person would have melted into the background at that point, so as not to attract further attention. Any sensible person would have got right out of Jerusalem, beyond the reaches of those who had marked his card. But Jesus does not do that. Instead, he adds fuel to the fire by coming out with something he knew would rankle them even more.

Reading: John 12:20–26

'Unless a grain of wheat falls to the earth and dies, it remains no more than a single grain. But if it does fall to the ground and die, it bears much fruit.' He's referring to his own death, and the fruit is the Movement, the Way, the Church, Christianity, which will grow out of his death when it comes.

- What will be the fruits of your death when it comes, as come it will?
- What will they say about you when you're gone?
- What mark will you have left on this world?
- What will the fruit of your living and dying on this earth actually be?

Have you ever thought of sitting down and writing your own obituary, as a little private exercise? But what would you write?

- She was a crabbit auld besom?
- He was a grumpy auld goat?
- She tried to make the world a better place?
- He did his best to live his life for other people?

I invite you to take some time now to think about what might be said about you when you're gone, and then to write down the most significant or most striking thought that comes into your head. Take the paper home with you, and look at it now and again. Use it to reflect on who you are, and what you are, or even what you might yet still become.

Time for reflection and writing

Song: 'Today I live, one day shall come my death' (CH4 725)

MAUNDY THURSDAY MEDITATION

This meditation leads directly into the sacrament of Holy Communion. Suggested music for the times of reflection: 'Gabriel's Oboe' by Ennio Morricone, from the film The Mission.

What is this Jesus thinking of?!

- He's scandalised everybody by kicking over their tables in the temple – and then he was spotted talking to a tree.
- He's been telling people that, if they wanted to, they could, with nothing but faith, make a mountain move itself into the sea.
- He said it was OK for a woman to squander an absolute fortune on the perfume she poured all over his feet.

And now, tonight, even when the writing's on the wall; even when he knows he's only got hours to live – and with all that's still to come – what does he go and do? He organises, of all things, a dinner party. What is this Jesus thinking of?!

Tonight let us try to understand the strangeness of this man. Tonight let us try to feel for what is in his mind. Tonight, in order to do that, I need to ask you to close your eyes now, and imagine – you are Jesus. Yes, that's right, I'm asking you to imagine you are Jesus himself. Your thoughts are his thoughts, and his thoughts are your thoughts, at least for a little while ...

You are Jesus, and you've come early to the upper room. The others haven't arrived yet. It is night time, and you've just climbed the outside stairs, and you open the door and look in. It's not a big room, and to be honest, it's quite gloomy. Only a few little oil lamps dotted around. But at least it's warm. And there's the table, all prepared: the bread and the wine ready for the meal.

Go in and close the door behind you, Jesus. It's been a hard day; you are tired. Sit down and rest your feet, and close your eyes. It is peaceful here, and quiet too in the time before the rest of them come. You have space to be alone with your thoughts. What are you thinking about, Jesus, as you sit there, alone in this room?

Time of reflection (play music)

What's going on in your mind, Jesus, knowing, as you do, the torture and the pain that lies ahead? Are you scared? And is there sadness too? You've tried to do your best for them, and now betrayal. Is that why you are hurting badly inside – because of the huge disappointment you feel? God knows, you've loved them in a way that nobody else could. But it's not only them – the whole world doesn't want you now. Are you feeling alone, Jesus, and lonely? And those tears in your eyes – are they tears of regret because it could all have been so different? Is that what you are thinking now?

Time of reflection (play music)

But you've always known it would be like this. Right from the beginning you knew this is how it would end. You've been faithful to God; faithful to them. You've said and done all the right things. But you were far too radical: they couldn't handle it. They would have had to change their ways completely; trusted you completely; and that would have meant turning everything on its head. But they weren't up to it. What a shame; it could have been so different. Are these your thoughts now, Jesus?

Time of reflection (play music)

Don't give up though, Jesus. You can fight against the despondency. You know you are to die; but you also know about the new kingdom and the glory that awaits. There's still time left before the cross. Still time to show them that, in the end, love will conquer evil; still time to convince them that death and separation are not all there is. Still time to tell them of another banquet and that they will all share in it. But how? How to tell them you are only the beginning of something greater; that a new agreement between God and his people has begun in you? How to tell them there's more: a new and different day? The bread, Jesus; the bread and the wine. Think hard, Jesus, think hard how you might do it.

Time of reflection (play music)

This meal you are about to share with them now: not just marking the Passover and looking back to the time God freed them from their slavery. Bless the bread, Jesus; it will become powerful; it will become more than bread. Say to them it stands for your body. The bread – it will mean you. Break the bread for them; and as they eat it, they'll remember you; they will become part of you and you part of them. They will feel that; and it will make a difference to them. As they eat the bread, you will be real to them, so they will know you are always with them.

And the wine, Jesus, think about the wine. Pour it out for them; this red wine: like your blood which tomorrow will flow as they put the nails in your hands. Tell them the wine is your blood; the blood which sustains your life. They will drink the red wine and they will make the connection. And so they will be able to share in your life. They will become part of you, and you part of them as they drink the red wine. And you will never die for them as long as they drink the wine. That will be real for them, Jesus. You will be real. So think hard. Think hard about the bread and the wine, and what it will mean.

Time of reflection (play music)

There are footsteps – a burst of laughter from the foot of the stairs. It must be Peter – he's always loud. And the voices of the others. Savour these last moments of being alone, Jesus. From now on it will be different. No more quiet times. You must wake up; your friends are here. They will want you to be their host, and they will be your guests. This is your table; this is your time. They will eat and drink with you, and from now on you will be real to them whenever they do that. Stir yourself, Jesus. The dreaming time is over. It is time now for the bread and wine ...

And so the disciples come through the door smiling. They are eager to greet their friend: the one who has given them so much; loved them so much; and will continue to mean so much to them, as heaven's eternal grace is revealed to them in the bread and the wine.

'Peace be with you, Jesus!' each one says. And he returns their greeting: 'Peace be with you too.' We'll do the same thing for each other now: 'Peace be with you.'

Sharing the peace

Introduction to the sacrament of Holy Communion

And so, on that night long ago, this strange man Jesus said and did the most inappropriate thing. But ever since then, his friends have taken him at his word, and have said and done the same thing. And because of this, they have understood his meaning, and felt his presence, and known his power operating in their lives. They have known the reality of the presence of the Jesus who died, but who rose from death, and is active and alive in their thinking and living.

Tonight then, he is the host and we are his guests. We who are his friends gather with him now, and in this sacred meal, Christ himself is with us in this bread and wine.

Share communion

A PASSOVER SEDER FOR MAUNDY THURSDAY

A number of people can be involved in the preparation and leading of this Seder meal, which takes place around a large table (or several small tables put together). Each individual place is set with a candle, a small plastic cup of wine, a baby-wipe, a sprig of parsley and a dish of salt, a small piece of homemade unleavened bread and a dish of horseradish sauce, and harosets (apples, nuts and raisins bound together with honey). A printed order of service (with responses, etc) is needed for each person. A child asks the questions. The meal leads into a celebration of the sacrament of Holy Communion.

Introduction

The sacrament of Holy Communion has its origin in the Jewish Passover Feast: the Passover Seder. Jesus was a Jew, and it was to mark this feast that he and his closest friends met in that upper room in Jerusalem.

They met to remember how their ancestors were once slaves in Egypt. So there was always an element of sadness in the meal. They met to give thanks to God who had freed his people from their slavery, and guided them through the desert to the Promised Land which became their new home. So there was always an element of gladness in the meal. And they met in expectation that God would continue to care for his people in the future as he had cared in the past. So there was always hope and confidence at the meal.

The Passover Feast was always ritualistic: the same ancient words were spoken; the same symbolic actions were always performed; the same food and drink were always on the table. Tonight we will follow some of that ritual: do the things that Jesus did; hear the same words that Jesus heard; taste the same kind of food that Jesus and his friends tasted.

We begin by singing Psalm 122, the song they always sang when they arrived in Jerusalem to celebrate the feast.

Song: 'I rejoiced when I heard them say' (CH4 83)

Lighting the candles

As the candles are lit, together let us bless the Lord our God:

All say:

BLESSED ARE YOU, OUR LORD AND GOD, RULER OF THE UNIVERSE,
FOR GIVING US FESTIVALS AND SEASONS FOR REJOICING,

AND FOR BRINGING US TO THIS TIME OF THE YEAR:
THE SPRINGTIME, THE SEASON OF OUR FREEDOM.

Prayer

Blessed are you, our Lord and God,
for bringing us together this night
to celebrate the Feast of Unleavened Bread.
As we gather here,
we are linked with the friends and families
who throughout the centuries
have celebrated this Passover festival.

We celebrate the springtime;
we celebrate the going out from Egypt;
we celebrate our freedom;
we celebrate our living, whose fullness is yours;
we celebrate our future, which rests with you alone.
And so we praise your holy name
for bringing us to this happy time;
this season of our freedom.

Together let us bless the Lord our God.

All raise their cups and say:

BLESSED ARE YOU, OUR LORD AND GOD

and then drink some wine.

The washing of hands

In preparation for this meal which we share,
we wash our hands:
a symbolic action of purification;
a token of our intention to be pure within ourselves.

All wash their hands with baby-wipes.

The questions

A young child asks:

Why is this night different from all other nights?

Why do we eat parsley tonight?

Why do we eat unleavened bread and bitter herbs tonight?

Why do we eat harosets tonight?

The reply

Our ancestors were slaves in the land of Egypt. The Eternal One, our God, brought us out from there with a strong hand and an outstretched arm.

Now if our God had not brought our fathers from Egypt, then we might still be there, enslaved to the Pharaoh in Egypt.

Long, long ago, our fathers worshipped idols. But now the Eternal One is our God and we worship him. It is as the Bible tells us: 'Thus says the God of Israel: "In the days of old your fathers lived beyond the river. They worshipped other gods. I took Abraham, your father, from beyond the river and led him through the whole land of Canaan. I increased his family by giving him a son, Isaac. And I gave Isaac two sons, Jacob and Esau. Jacob and his sons went down to Egypt".'

Blessed be God who keeps his promises to Israel. For God foretold the end of the bondage. God said to Abraham: 'Know that you and your children will be strangers in a strange land. They will be enslaved there and oppressed for four hundred years. The people who oppress them, however, will be judged. Afterwards they will come forth with great wealth.'

Together let us bless the Lord our God.

All lift their cups and say:

THE PROMISE MADE TO OUR FATHERS
HOLDS TRUE FOR US TODAY.

All take a sip of wine.

The story (Exodus 12:1–17, 29–36)

Our victory is diminished because of the death of our foes. Let us all spill a few drops of wine onto our plates in compassion for those who were slain that night.

All spill a few drops of wine.

Together let us thank the Lord our God

All say:

HOW THANKFUL WE MUST BE TO YOU, OUR GOD,
THE ALL-PRESENT ONE,
FOR THE GOOD YOU DO TO YOUR PEOPLE.

Eating the green vegetables

We eat this green vegetable, a fruit of the earth. We recall that our ancestors were tillers of the soil, grateful for God's bounties. But in dipping the vegetable into the salt, we remember, too, the tears which our ancestors shed while suffering the hardness of slavery. May our gratitude for the blessings we enjoy help to soften the pain of sorrow, and convert tears to joy and gladness.

Together let us bless the Lord our God.

All say:

BLESSED ARE YOU, OUR LORD AND GOD,
CREATOR OF THE FRUITS OF THE EARTH

then dip the parsley in salt before eating it.

Eating the unleavened bread and bitter herbs

This is the bread of affliction
which our fathers ate in the land of Egypt.
Because there was no free time to wait for the dough to be leavened,
they baked cakes of unleavened bread.
We dip the unleavened bread in the bitter herb, the horseradish,
recalling how the Egyptians embittered the lives
of our ancestors with hard work.
Let us eat the bread of affliction.

All dip the bread in the horseradish and eat it.

Eating the harosets

The haroset is a mixture of apples, nuts, raisins and honey.
It represents the mortar our ancestors used for bricklaying
when they were slaves.
For us, it is a reminder that the freedom
we are celebrating today is also hard work.

Let us take the harosets together.

All eat the harosets.

Personal deliverance

In every generation, each person must look on themselves
as having come out of Egypt personally.
For it was not our fathers alone
whom the Holy One (blessed be his name) redeemed.
With them, he redeemed us too.
So in this spirit we see ourselves
as participants in the Exodus.

All say:

AS INHERITORS OF THE PRICELESS HERITAGE OF LIBERTY,
WE JOIN NOW IN PRAISING AND GLORIFYING GOD'S HOLY NAME,
REMEMBERING THE TASK IS OURS
TO WORK FOR THE LIBERTY OF GOD'S PEOPLE TODAY:
THOSE WHO ARE BOUND BY CHAINS OF POVERTY AND INJUSTICE,
AND KEPT PRISONER BY SLAVE-MASTERS
WHOSE FIRST PRIORITY IS TO EXPLOIT AND CONTROL.

FOR THE MIRACLES WROUGHT BY GOD IN THE PAST,
AS WELL AS IN OUR DAY,
WE OFFER OUR THANKFULNESS.

FOR GOD HAS DELIVERED US FROM SLAVERY TO FREEDOM:
FROM SORROW TO HAPPINESS;
FROM MOURNING TO REJOICING;
FROM DARKNESS TO LIGHT.

IN GRATITUDE FOR THESE BLESSINGS,
WE SHALL SING SONGS OF PRAISE,
AND WE SHALL DRINK THE CUP OF BLESSING.

All take a sip of wine.

Then, with a new song, and a renewed flavour,
let us give thanks once again
for our physical deliverance and our spiritual freedom.

All say:

BLESSED ARE YOU OUR GOD,
WHO HAS REDEEMED YOUR PEOPLE.
BLESSED ARE YOU,
GREAT SOVEREIGN OF THE UNIVERSE,
WHO CREATED THE FRUIT OF THE VINE.

Song: 'Praise God, for he is kind' (CH4 92)

The sacrament of Holy Communion

SYMBOLIC ACTIONS FOR GOOD FRIDAY

These symbolic actions can be used to complete Good Friday worship. A flower on a short stem (wild flowers from the garden), a small glass of wine mixed with vinegar, and a twig are placed by each person's seat prior to the service. The worship leader will need a small supply of fragrant oil (e.g. lavender oil) for making the sign of the cross.

The flower (the destruction)

I invite you now to take into your hands the flower.
Take a moment to examine the great beauty there.
Notice the delicacy, the shape, the balance,
the texture, the colour, the symmetry ...

(Pause)

What kind of genius mind
lies behind this wondrous creation?
What kind of artist could shape this intricate design?
What kind of love, to have gifted humanity
with something so precious?
And what kind of generosity,
to enhance our experience with this beautiful thing
and help make our living so rich and so full?

In the quietness here, will you give thanks to God
for the gentle beauty you hold now in your hands?

(Pause)

Now, on the evening of this bad Friday,
crush this flower with your fingers.
On this bad Friday, tear and destroy it.
On this bad Friday, however reluctant,
however unwilling,
turn into waste this living beauty you now hold.

As I speak, waste it well;
destroy it beyond recognition,
until what is left is no longer beautiful;
until what is left is bruised and damaged and broken,
until what is left is nasty, and ugly, and dead.

And in this action, as you make the obvious connection,
destroy it until it can no longer delight;
no longer please; no longer hold blessing;
no longer hold the grace and benediction of highest heaven.
And when you have finished, lay this thing down,
and ask God, the generous one, to forgive you
for the terrible destruction you have done,
for something of beauty itself has been removed from the world tonight.
And pray that Christ, in his great love, and in his compassion,
will have mercy on your mind and your soul.

Choir: 'Jesus, remember me' (CH4 775)

The wine and the vinegar (the cost)

And now the wine,
which has been mixed with a little vinegar.
It will leave a bitter taste.
It stands for the cost – the cost to our God,
and not least, the cost to ourselves –
of the dreadful destruction
we remember on this fateful day.

But the bitter taste of this wine and vinegar
also represents the daily re-enactments of that crucifixion,
since, in the brokenness of our humanity,
we repeatedly fail, and fall short of heaven's intention
(though heaven well understands
we can do nothing other than this,
for each one of us is human and not divine).
And so heaven understands; heaven understands;
heaven understands what it is to be you and to be me.
Even so, the cost remains:
a world containing less love than it ought:
less generosity and less tolerance;
less warmth and less acceptance;
less justice and less equal sharing;
less building-up, less interconnection;
less happiness, less compassion, less peace.

In the brokenness,
which is the eternal condition of our earthly humanity,
we harm ourselves, and break the heart of the God who weeps;
the God whose greatest wish for all his people is fullness of living:
freedom, and plenty for all, and life that is complete.

So let us drink the bitter wine together,
and in the silence take time to reflect
on how the human race is foolish,
and on how the price of our imperfection is heavy and hard.

(Pause)

Choir: 'Jesus, remember me'

The twig (the forgiveness)

Now take into your hands the twig.
Feel the random roughness;
the coarse and uneven texture.
And make this obvious connection:
a twig that is wood: a cross of wood.
And both of them, in their own way,
representing a lifetime's regret for wrongdoing.

The twig stands for the things you know
you have done and wish you had not.
It stands for the secrets of your heart
you are too scared to mention.
It stands for the thoughts of your mind
which are too embarrassing to share;
too problematic to reveal;
too hurtful to recall.

Look at yourself, your character, your personality,
and identify those things you wish were just not there.

(Pause)

Once upon a time, you pretended not to notice,
and looked the other way
when you could have eased
someone else's difficulty.
Another time, you deliberately set out to wound,
and your words were intended to damage.
More than once, you kept what you had for yourself:
refusing to share, preferring to hoard up,
in the face of hardship and hunger and need.
You kept your head down
when it was your rightful purpose to defend and protect.
And there are other secrets too,
which only you know, and only God knows:
secrets which will go with you to your grave.

(Pause)

Now is the time, and this is the place.
On this Good Friday,
break this twig into many small pieces.
Break it so it is no more a twig
and until each part becomes
unrecognisable and insignificant.
For this represents the forgiveness of the God of heaven;
forgiveness which is always total,
always comprehensive, always complete.

For those who acknowledge
the brokenness of their own humanity;
for those who recognise they have made the living of others
less than it should be;
for those who are sorry they have a hand
in the crucifixion of the innocent,
God snaps into pieces every last regret;
counts those faults as if they had never been;
ashes to ashes, dust to dust;
returning to the earth from which they came.

And this is the Good News
of the cross that's made of wood:
no record is kept; the slate is wiped clean.
The forgiveness of this Good Friday
is for you and for me.

(Pause)

Choir: 'Jesus, remember me'

The oil (the mending)

And finally, there is oil:
the gentle oil that makes for healing;
the healing oil that makes for calming;
the calming oil that mends our brokenness;
the oil that soothes;
the oil that bestows blessing;
the oil of peace.

Earth is here and heaven is here,
and the distance between them is very thin.
Tonight there is grief: the oil will soothe it.
Tonight there is regret: the oil will calm it.
Tonight there is despondency: the oil will relieve it.
Tonight there is danger and wondering:
the oil will give reassurance and hope.

For we are unlike those first folk
who stood trembling at the foot of the cross,
and witnessed him struggling painfully
as he drew his last breath.
They believed the one they loved was gone for ever.
But we have the benefit of history and hindsight,
and so we know the sadness of this solemn night
will lead to the joy and the light of the morning.

For we know:

'Goodness is stronger than evil;
love is stronger than hate.
Light is stronger than darkness;
life is stronger than death.
People of God, victory is ours;
victory is ours through him who loves us.' (Desmond Tutu)

And so, I invite those who want to
to come forward and kneel in humility
to receive the mark of the cross of Jesus the Christ,
which will be placed on your forehead with a little oil.

It stands for the God who died,
the God who rose,
the God who lives again,
the God whose love is for you,
and whose love is for ever and for always.

There is no benediction
for the people of God on this night,
so once you have received this sign and symbol,
will you leave this place in silence,
and will you leave this place in peace?

Folk come forward to receive the sign of the cross ...

WHY DID YOU HAVE TO DIE?

Voice 1:

Why did you have to die like that?

Voice 2:

Why did you voluntarily arrange your own suicide?

Voice 1:

Couldn't you have found another way to make your point?

Voice 2:

Why did your story have to end
with the pain of nails through your flesh,
and the death by inches of slow self-suffocation?

Voice 1:

'A glorious death,' some of them say,
but I'm certain you didn't think so at the time.

Voice 2:

'To redeem the humanity that you love'
is what they tell me,
but surely you didn't have to go to such an extreme.

Voice 1:

'To win victory over evil' is the popular rumour,
but others have taken a stand for what was good, what was right,
and they didn't end up on a cross.

Voice 2:

'A sacrifice to the Devil's demands' is the theory.
But if the Devil could insist on your life,
then that makes him more powerful than the God of heaven.

Voice 1:

Jesus, why did you have to die like that?
What was your bright idea and purpose
when you volunteered to end it all and breathe your last?

Voice 2:

Could it be you were showing
the extent of your love for us?

Voice 1:

Could it be that you wanted to demonstrate
the length you were prepared to go?

Voice 2:

Could it be that, in the end,
you chose to forget yourself:
to forget yourself for us;
to forget yourself for all;
to forget yourself for me?

Voice 1:

What wondrous love is this,
O my soul, O my soul?
What wondrous love is this
that in my humanity I am trying to understand?

Voice 2:

Jesus, I'll never be able to understand you.

Voice 1:

I'll never be able to come to terms with who you are.

Voice 2:

In the face of your love,
my words are futile and wholly inadequate.

Voice 1:

In the force of such love,
perhaps my silence is the only way to respond.

Time of quiet

Voice 2:

Inscribed upon the cross,
we see in shining letters: *God is love.*

Voice 1:

For being who you are and loving me like that,
blessing and honour, and glory and power be unto you.

EASTER

THE ROCK

You know, I was no ordinary rock. I mean, I don't really come off right in those stories. No, it wasn't like I was just shoved in front of a hole.

I was special: sculpted and crafted every bit as carefully as that cross they hung him on. They'd smoothed my hard, weathered edges so I'd roll. Then they'd struggled under my weight, dug trenches for me to follow up the hill a little ways, and nailed pegs in the ground so I'd stay put until it was time. And I was huge: a giant turned into a tool designed to keep things out and in.

They'd carried his broken body into the tomb as the sun set on Friday night and placed it, lifeless, on one of my brother stones. Then it was my turn. After they'd removed the pegs, and I'd found *my* final resting place, nobody was gonna turf me out of the way. I knew my job. I closed things up, put a final end to things. I was the seal … rock solid … immovable. That was me.

Well, that's what you'd think, wouldn't you? That's what anyone would expect. But then, we'd had dealings with him before:

- In the beginning, we'd been putty in his hands: the stuff of creation, and we'd given way then.

- When the Israelites were thirsty in the desert, the order had been given to strike us and we'd give water. We obeyed.

- Into stones as solid as me had been chiselled truths so eternal that they would echo down time long after the original stones had turned to dust and blown away.

We'd even had personal encounters with the one I wouldn't be able to hold:

- He'd been tempted to turn us into bread, but he'd known that life was more than just existing.

- And later on, he'd challenged men to be the first to cast us if they were innocent, and they threw us away.

- Only a few days ago, the powerful who silenced him were told we would shout aloud if his followers were stopped.

I knew my job. I closed things up, put a final end to things. I was the seal: rock solid; immovable; that was me. Well, that's what you'd think, wouldn't you?

But there is something far more powerful than me: something that can never be closed up or ended; one thing that is truly immovable. In this Jesus Christ, I met my match and my Maker. He moved me, and he'll move you too.

Sally Foster-Fulton

FARTHING WOOD

Voice 1:

As was their custom, the animals gathered in a convenient clearing in the forest on what they regarded as a particularly special day of the year. There were other opportunities to meet at other times of course, but some didn't see their getting together regularly as all that vital, or they couldn't be bothered, or they weren't really all that interested anyway. But this day was a special day, so special efforts had been made all round.

Voice 2:

This kind of gathering had gone on for generation after generation – ever since their Great Leader had died, and that was centuries ago. He had shown them a very different way to live, and always spoke about their need to look out for each other and not only be concerned for their own personal interests. He was very influential, and attracted a lot of interest because of his charisma. But it wasn't only that. He taught them a method of how to be at peace with themselves, and at peace with their world. In the things he did, and the way he was, Great Leader was perceived to be the ultimate living example of how the very essence of goodness itself could dramatically change the way things are, so that everyone could live in harmony, side by side.

Voice 3:

Now, although Great Leader had died a long, long time ago, the animals claimed he was actually still very much alive. They said this partly because their ancient writings stated that, after his death, he was seen and heard by his closest friends: indeed, on more than one occasion, he was said to have actually shared a meal with them. And that is very, very strange, because, as we all know, dead bodies in general don't walk and talk, and they have absolutely no need to take in food.

Voice 1:

All this talk about Great Leader dying and coming to life again, and still being alive and with them, was quite confusing for many of the animals. For some of them it was a very difficult reality to understand.

Voice 2:

The sheep, for example, who were not terribly well-noted for their powers of intelligence, chose to interpret this idea of his continued existence in a strictly physical sense. They thought that, nowadays, Great Leader lived in the great sheep-fold in the sky where he watched over the world with eyes that could see what everybody was doing, and ears that could hear what everybody was saying.

The sheep believed Great Leader made it his business to interfere directly in the affairs and events of the world on a minute-by-minute basis, and cause certain things to happen, and appoint the precise moment when one of their number should die, while allowing others, whose time he had decided was not yet up, to carry on living. So 'coincidence' wasn't a word in the sheep vocabulary. Everything was regulated and controlled. They operated on the basis that, when they did die, they would be physically transported in an upward direction to the most idyllic green pasture imaginable, where they would munch and chomp to their heart's content on the finest grass for ever and eternity.

Well, sheep will be sheep, and that was what they believed. Even so, their understanding seemed to serve them well, for in a limited way, it allowed them to make sense of the really big questions about life and death, and the future that lay in store at the end of the day.

Voice 3:

The foxes, on the other hand – a bit more crafty, far less gullible and accepting of simplistic, face-value explanations – thought the sheep had a fairly primitive and superficial understanding of what was meant by Great Leader's continuing to live after he had died.

The foxes looked for his existence in what we might call a supernatural context. According to them, Great Leader's physical flesh and bone did not reconstitute itself after his death. Instead, they believed it was his residual spirit, some form of invisible personal essence, an entity, which continued to remain alive. In some respects, the foxes weren't all that far away from what the sheep believed, because they also thought this spirit had volition, reasoning powers; a mind that was able to discern and choose, and having chosen, could intervene directly in events and situations.

So the foxes believed in a living, 'able-to-do-things' spirit, but it was that very word 'spirit' that foxed them, for they thought Great Leader now was some kind of ghost, albeit a holy one. But like the sheep, that was how they were able to make sense of things, and their more sophisticated understanding allowed them to work out their place in the world, and how they fitted into the order of the great, big complicated scheme of things.

Voice 1:

Now, owls are much respected, because everybody knows they are the wisest of creatures. Owls can see behind and beneath what others might accept as straightforward and obvious. So the owls adopted a cleverer, if admittedly more complicated and harder to grasp approach to what is meant by the idea that Great Leader is still alive.

Voice 2:

'Owl,' said one of the sheep. 'Tell us why you object so much to our way of thinking?'

Voice 1:

'Well, it's like this,' replied the owl patiently (for he'd been over all this with these sheep a hundred times before). 'Subscribing to a theory that dead bodies can come alive involves suspending all rationality and reason. You see, Great Leader was a human being in every possible respect. He came from a woman's womb; he knew the pain of a nail when it was hammered into his hand. Just because he was great, it doesn't follow his physical body had special privileges which allowed it to contradict every law of science and nature. When Great Leader drew his last breath, as far as his body was concerned, that was it. The flesh decayed, and eventually returned to dust, as is the fate of every creature who lives in this world. So I'm sorry, sheep, but your understanding is lacking and just won't do.'

Voice 3:

'That's right, Owl,' said one of the fox brothers. 'A physical presence, either on this earth or living up in the sky, is ludicrous and laughable. Those daft sheep haven't got a clue. They've just accepted what they've been told, hook, line and sinker, and they don't have the sense to scratch beneath the surface to try to work out for themselves what the ancient story says and means.'

Voice 1:

'Hang on a minute, Fox,' responded the owl. 'I wouldn't be so smug if I were you, for your argument about spectres and ghosts stretches credibility beyond its limits as well.'

Voice 3:

'Oh really?' said Fox. 'Well, if you're so clever, how do you explain the bit where it says that, after his death, Great Leader appeared, and sat down and shared a meal with some of his friends? Are you saying our holy scriptures aren't true?'

Voice 1:

'Fox,' said Owl, with an even more patient smile on his beak. 'Again you have to resort to suspending credibility and reason to believe things took place in the way it says. Have you never heard anything about bereavement and the grieving process? Do you not know that a profound sense of loss, such as Great Leader's contemporaries experienced in the weeks and months following his death, can do very funny things to the mind? Any psychologist or any priest will tell you that it is extremely common for people who long to see someone who has died – to see them.

'Or if they are pining hard enough, to hear the voice they loved so well, or even feel a touch on the shoulder, or hear a footstep on the stairs. These are the kind of sensory experiences that many creatures have, and they are very real to the individual at the time. But they are only mind projections all the same. So this strange, unrecognisable, ghost-like character which his two friends said they met on the road to Emmaus: in their grief, in their great trauma, he *seemed* very real to them. But then this episode passed, because, as it says, "eventually their eyes were opened, and he disappeared from their sight".

'No, Fox, the notion that ghosts, spectres and spirits which inhabit the ether take on the appearance of a creature will not do either. And you don't need to resort to the supernatural when trying to persuade yourself that Great Leader is still alive.'

Voice 4:

'Eh, excuse me, Mr Owl,' said a little voice located high up in the branch of a tree. It was a squirrel who had been listening attentively to all this conversation. 'I think I know the reason why we can say Great Leader is still with us.'

Voice 1:

'Oh, really,' said the owl, a bit put out at the audacity of this young squirrel who was actually quite junior in the pecking order, and should have had more respect for his elders and betters. 'Go on then, give us the benefit of your wisdom and tell us.'

Voice 4:

'Well,' piped up the squirrel, the confidence of youth allowing him to be bold as brass. 'It all has to do with what we mean when we use this word "spirit". A spirit isn't a body, so of course the sheep are barking up the wrong tree. And for foxes to say that spirits (good or evil) inhabit the atmosphere around us is nothing more than vivid imagination and superstition.

'But, Mr Owl, what if the word spirit is used in a different way: as in the spirit of compassion; the spirit of generosity; the spirit of forgiveness, and so on. These are all invisible forces, and there's no denying they do exist, and have power, because we've seen that with our own eyes many a time. But they're not flesh and blood, like a body. And they're not ghosts or spectres either.

'And what if we gather all these great influences together, and sum them up by calling them the "Spirit of living Love"? Isn't that who Great Leader is? And don't our scriptures actually say: "God is Love"? And isn't that how we can say Great Leader is always alive and with us? Love, not dying on a cross all those years ago, but Love living inside you and inside me.'

Voice 1:

'Hmph!' said the owl, still put out by this young whippersnapper squirrel's precociousness, but even so, still gracious enough to say: 'I guess I couldn't have put it better myself.'

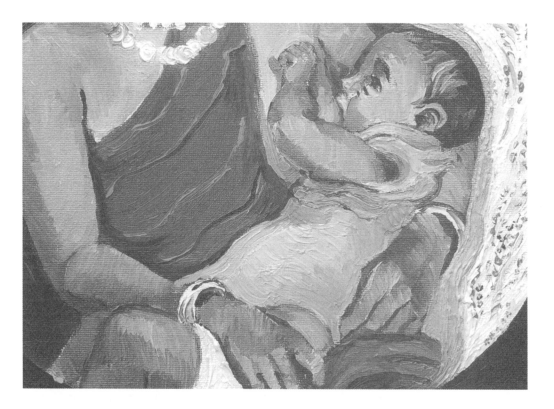

A FLIGHT OF FANCY

Part 1: Welcome aboard

Good morning, ladies and gentlemen. This is your captain speaking. I'd like to welcome you aboard this Sunday morning flight. This journey we make will be a long one: in fact, it will last for many years. But we will try to do everything possible to make the experience pleasant and enjoyable.

We realise many of you have done a lot of travelling before, but for your own well-being, and for the benefit of your fellow passengers, can I ask you to listen very carefully for the next few minutes, and to pay close attention to the following advice and information, which we believe will enhance everyone's experience as we travel together.

Firstly, I am required to draw your attention to the exit routes, clearly identifiable by red carpet, because this journey, like any other, is not without its dangers and difficulties. The best way of dealing with these though, and the most effective method of getting the very best out of your travel with us, is to follow the company rules. The rule book is large and can be very complicated.

Reading: Romans 5:1–11 (GNB)

Part 2: Important travel information

You will have noticed that part of these regulations is about being considerate to those around you. That's what the references to this man called Jesus Christ dying for others are all about; the bit where it says: 'He made us his friends through the death of his Son.' This is about God putting his own priorities second in order to make life easier for people.

Admittedly it was always a struggle for Jesus, as it always is for us. There are bound to be those who travel with us whom we might not particularly take to. And of course, there are others who, for one reason or another, will always need our help. But we would all be well-advised to try to follow his example. In our case we'll probably not need to die for others. In fact, we'll be of more use living for them. And if you do that, then I am confident you will never have any reason to use the escape routes at all.

You must have noticed by now that the seat you are in is not the most comfortable. We are very aware of this. However, there's a sense in which the seats were never meant to be totally comfortable, nor is sitting in them ever a guarantee of trouble-free travel. They offer no protection against illness, upset or even personal tragedy on this particular journey. Indeed the World Health Organisation has asked us to point out the specific risk of DVT: deep vein thrombosis, a problem caused by remaining seated in the same position for too long. Their best advice is that problems can be avoided by not sitting still. They say you should be active and on the move. You can be sure our crew will encourage you in this, and perhaps suggest what you can do and how you might do it. They're not experts, by any manner of means, but they will have given this a lot of thought and practice.

Our flight path will take us through a wide range of weather conditions. Air traffic control says we can expect it to be very turbulent and bumpy at times as we encounter strong headwinds and storms. It has to be said these do often cause great distress and fear among passengers, but unfortunately there is no way of avoiding them during our travel. For the most part these are usually only temporary.

Sometimes we will climb to the heights, leaving the dark clouds behind us. Those seasoned travellers among you will have had that experience before and therefore will know it is there that you will find great satisfaction simply in being. You will also be inspired by the beauty of what you see outside, which has been especially created for your pleasure. But you will discover most of your fulfilment will come from what you sense and experience inside this environment: the things that come from those who share your journey with you.

Under your seat you will find a life jacket, which you must put on quickly should an emergency arise. Never be reluctant to do that. In the past, some determinedly independent people have presumed that they themselves had all the personal resources they required to deal with any crises. That is a very big mistake, and several avoidable tragedies have occurred as a result. Your crew will always respond willingly to your requests for assistance. In fact, they particularly want to do that, so don't be reluctant to call on them in times of distress. Similarly, in a crisis situation, oxygen masks will drop automatically. Help, therefore, is never far away. And it is available permanently, completely free of charge.

Of course, it is entirely up to you whether you choose to reach out and take advantage of what is rightfully intended for you. But in that connection, let me say our experience is that you can depend not only on crew members, but on fellow travellers as well. If you find you are in distress, you will discover your companions will also encourage you with their own strength and confidence and experience. So, from the assistance available around you and above you then, you are never entirely on your own.

Shortly after take-off, the crew will be serving complimentary drinks from the bar, red wine, which will accompany the meal, which in itself is rather special on this trip. Eating and drinking together on this particular journey has been found to have very great power. It was introduced as a feature many years ago by a man who saw it as a kind of farewell dinner. But ever since then it has had the effect of drawing people together in a clever and subtle way. Nobody quite understands why, but it is as if the spirit and influence of its inventor is still alive and present today, accompanying us on our journey. And his influence is still so strong that, simply by eating together, the love he had for everyone then is curiously rekindled in folk now.

It works to neutralise the inevitable annoyances, grumpiness and ill-natured antagonism that most people experience as a natural consequence of their long and tiring journey together. But time and again, the meal seems to cut through all this, and allows travellers to co-exist in peace even more closely than before.

But the other important feature of this sharing is the feeling it creates: a feeling of unity and commonality of purpose. So the meal is worth looking forward to, and the crew have taken the trouble to invite you personally, because they themselves are convinced its beneficial power is freely available to everyone who joins in it.

Having said that, however, I do need to warn you about our sweet trolley. There you'll discover all sorts of temptations in their most exquisite and refined form. Most popular seems to be 'Death by Chocolate', which is tantalising and quite irresistible. But we do offer an alternative. To be honest with you, it is rarely as rich or attractive; in fact, it's no more than a fatless sponge. On the menu it goes by the name of 'Life by Love'.

Admittedly it is a strange name for a cake, but this was Jesus' favourite. It was his first choice every time. Jesus knew the unhealthiness there is in always submitting to the craving for what is outwardly attractive and instantly gratifying. He once spent 40 days in the dessert(!), and there he concluded that transient satisfaction is not real satisfaction at all; that the more fulfilling option is often found in what is seemingly less attractive. So if you want to be like him, you'll need to choose 'Life by Love', for that's always where the best reward is found.

Finally, just a quick word about our destination. As far as we know, it is an idyllic place; reportedly more wonderful than we can ever imagine. Vast numbers have made the journey there before you, and when you arrive, you will have the opportunity of meeting with them again.

Unfortunately there are no maps showing us the route. But Jesus makes it possible; he was the first to journey into this great unknown. He was the pioneer whose footsteps we can follow, and who demonstrated that all the hassle of our arduous trip is rewarding and worthwhile.

But don't forget the meal: let the love and the sharing work to help you. For it is only when we allow his living spirit of love to shape who we are that the journey of life becomes the pleasure it was always meant to be.

JESUS AND ELVIS

Voice 1:

On that first Easter morning, they went to the tomb and found it was empty. There were stories about conspiracy and theft, but that was some time after the event: not right away, and certainly not first thing on Easter morning. The first ones to arrive did not immediately think Jesus' body had been stolen. Instead, we hear of them running back to the other disciples to report the body was *missing*.

In present-day terms, I guess it would be like you or me visiting a funeral parlour, being shown into the viewing room, and discovering an empty coffin. And if that did happen, it's hardly likely that our *first* thought would be that a theft had taken place. More probably we would assume that the undertakers had made a bad mistake, and that we'd been shown into the wrong room: the body must be somewhere else in the building.

Voice 2:

I've never been to Memphis, Tennessee to visit the grave of Elvis Presley, but anybody who *has* been there will know that the grave in the cemetery where Elvis was originally buried is now empty. Some years ago, there was serious concern that the more fanatical of his fans would indulge in a bit of modern-day body-snatching, so the remains were moved for safekeeping to the high-security grounds of Graceland, his estate. However, apparently there was uproar in some quarters when this happened, because many who made a pilgrimage to his grave did, in fact, genuinely believe that Elvis had been stolen.

Voice 1:

There is no shortage of theories about what happened to Jesus' body, and people have argued about it for centuries. Some say the Romans stole it, so the tomb wouldn't be a constant visual reminder that they had put this much-acclaimed popular hero to death.

In Riga, the capital city of Latvia, there stands the massive Freedom Monument. All around the base, the stonework is pock-marked with indentations made by bullets which came from Soviet rifles. The guns had been fired at Latvian patriots who, during the Soviet occupation of their country, risked their lives (and indeed, many lost their lives) as they attempted to lay flowers at the foot of the monument as a visible sign of resistance. So the Romans stole the body because they didn't want Jesus' tomb to provide that same kind of nationalistic focus. At least, that's one theory.

Voice 2:

Others argue it was the religious people who were responsible. It was the temple priests who arranged for the body to disappear, because they didn't want people deserting their Jewish religion to follow this new way preached and promoted by Jesus of Nazareth. The sooner he was forgotten the better as far as they were concerned, and the very last thing they wanted was for his tomb to become a shrine which would encourage his memory to be kept alive. If it was the temple authorities who had the body removed, then they made a big mistake, for their plan backfired on them. Jesus is probably the most remembered individual in the entire long history of this world.

Voice 1:

Another idea is that it was actually some of the disciples who performed the vanishing act. They crept back to the tomb in the middle of the night and removed the body so that folk would be convinced Jesus had indeed risen from the grave. In order to prove Jesus was God incarnate, they thought they'd give him a helping hand. So they *made* the body disappear. If that's what happened, then their ploy really did work, because ever since, a significant number of people have based their faith on an empty tomb, and on a corpse which somehow came back to life again.

Voice 2:

But whether any or none of these theories about the case of the missing body are true or false, it doesn't actually matter. For our understanding of what resurrection means, and our faith in a living, ever-present God does not depend, and never has, on any of this. There are other, more compelling reasons to proclaim that Christ is alive this Easter Day.

Voice 1:

Let's go back to Elvis Presley again, or 'Elvis the king', as his devotees like to call him. He died decades ago, yet still has a massive following which runs to tens of thousands of people.

We could legitimately draw certain parallels between Elvis and Jesus:

- both came from very ordinary, humble backgrounds

- both were highly controversial figures in their time

- both of them deeply upset the establishment by their new ways and unconventional behaviour

- both men died when they were young.

But perhaps the most significant similarity is the continuing massive effect each of their deaths has had on individuals:

- Still thousands of Elvis' followers come together on a regular basis to remember and celebrate and venerate their rock-star hero. You could be forgiven for calling it worship.

- Still parents name their children after him; while others go around dressed like him, and get their hair cut in that distinctive Elvis-style.

- Still there are those who do not believe Elvis Presley is dead at all – for his grave is now empty. The great king lives; his spirit is alive ...

Voice 2:

It is possible to say that in a very tangible and very real sense Elvis Presley is not dead and gone:

- Still he influences folk.

- Still he affects and inspires and changes people ...

Does this help us to understand what the resurrection of Jesus of Nazareth means and is? On a scale which is in no way comparable, and in no way compatible with Elvis Presley, the even more powerful influence of Jesus working in you and me. The living, lively, active spirit of Jesus operating in millions of people on this earth – and not just for the past few decades, but for the past 2000 years. And is this how, on this Easter morning, we have every good reason to make the claim that Jesus has died; Christ is risen; Christ is alive and well?

Voice 1:

What convinced those first disciples that their friend had resurrected to a new kind of life was not an empty tomb. That proved absolutely nothing. Instead, it was the reality of the challenging and comforting spirit of Jesus Christ which they continued to encounter in their living experience.

Voice 2:

It was the living spirit of Jesus which nudged them, and said: 'You have to share what you have so that the quality of other folk's living experience can be richer and fuller, just as heaven intends.'

Voice 1:

It was the continuing presence of this influential spirit of Jesus, and not his resuscitated, decaying corpse, which fired them up, and gave them the energy to establish his

Church: his new Body; his living Body of people here on earth.

Voice 2:

It is the continuing, active spirit of Jesus now – despite the cross; beyond the tomb; regardless of the disappearance of the body – which proves beyond any shadow of doubt that Love is indestructible – that it is the most powerful force we know, for even when faced with death itself, it survives.

Voice 1:

But not only that: it is the living spirit of Jesus alive now which proves that Love is eternal; Love is everlasting; Love never dies.

Voice 2:

Proof of this resurrection of Jesus is really very, very simple. You are here and I am here, and that can only mean Christ is not dead.

Voice 1:

You are here and I am here, which proves the King is alive and well.

RESURRECTION STORIES

Narrator:

I want you to listen to a story: a pretty hard-to-believe, unlikely story. Some people have difficulty believing it to be true. Others say it is no more than an idle tale.

Reading: Luke 24:1–12

Narrator:

Here are some other stories now. You might be one of those who think they also are hard to believe.

Reading: Luke 8:40–42, 49–55

A young girl:

When folk first heard what he did for me, most thought it was an idle tale. The mourners at our gate even stopped their weeping to laugh and mock him when he said I was only sleeping. They thought I was dead, you know. I'd been so sick for so long that everyone said there was no hope for me. I lived from my bed and listened to whispers: 'What a shame.' 'Poor little lamb.' 'It's God's will.'

But it seems this Jesus had other plans for me: he was a man of life, not death. He took me by the hand and told me to get up, to eat, to live. And I did! And here I am to tell the tale. Who knows what my life will be?

It's a great adventure and it's a gift. I can tell you one thing though: I won't waste it or take it for granted. And I'll always thank God for it because life is God's will. Jesus gave me my life back, so when I heard the 'tale' about him, I wasn't so doubtful, because I guess I was kind of resurrected too.

Reading: John 8:1–11

A woman:

If I'd heard the story of what he did for me, I'd have thought it was an idle tale. Things like that just don't happen in the real world. I'd been caught red-handed, as it were, and the fact that it takes two to tango didn't seem to matter to the crowd at the temple – especially to the 'holy men'.

This Jesus was teaching a crowd. Everyone was listening to him, and I think that's what had put the scribes and Pharisees in such a foul mood. They were out for blood, and if they couldn't have his, mine would do. I don't know who thought of it first, but I heard them whispering amongst themselves: 'Take her to him.' 'Let's see him get out of this one.' 'Let's see what his God's will would be.' So they made me stand in front of all those people and they humiliated me. I was made to feel subhuman.

They asked him what should be done with me. Should I be stoned, as the Law of Moses calls for? There was silence: he said nothing. Then he just bent down and drew in the sand. You could have heard a pin drop.

Just as the silence was becoming unbearable, he stood up and said it. You know the words ... you've heard my story: 'Let anyone of you who is without sin be the very first to throw a stone at her.' And then it happened. They simply walked away: every single one of them, until I was the only one left.

I just stood there. I waited. I needed something more, and he gave it to me.

'Has no one condemned you?' he asked.

'No one, sir,' I replied.

'Well then, neither do I. Go and sin no more.'

He gave me my life back, so when I heard the 'tale' about him, I wasn't so doubtful, because, you know this? I was resurrected too.

Reading: Matthew 19:16–22

A young man:

When folk hear what he said to me, most of them think that I was one of his rare failures. They think he didn't convince me or change me or save me. And I can understand that because, you see, I walked away. I couldn't handle what he had to say, what he asked me to do.

I'd been a good Jew all my life: I followed all the rules as best I could. And I studied, and I listened. That's why I went to him in the first place. I'd been listening to him and I was intrigued by what I heard. I suppose I wanted to know what he thought of me. Maybe deep down I wanted him to tell me that I'd made it: that there wasn't anything else for me to do. But he saw straight through me. 'If you wish to be perfect, go and sell all your possessions. Give the money to the poor and then you will have treasure in heaven. And then after that come and follow me.'

Talk about taking the wind out of your sails! I'm a rich man. I have a lot of things. So I walked away. I couldn't handle what he had to say, what he asked me to do. So folk think I was one of his rare failures ... that he didn't convince me or change me or save me.

Now, I can understand that, but there's a little point everyone seems to miss in my story. I went away right enough, but I went away grieving. And the grieving was the beginning of a change. It has taken some time, but I'm becoming convinced. I'm changing, and he did save me. Jesus showed me what life is really about. So when I heard the 'tale' about him, I wasn't so doubtful because I guess I'm kind of being resurrected too.

Sally Foster-Fulton

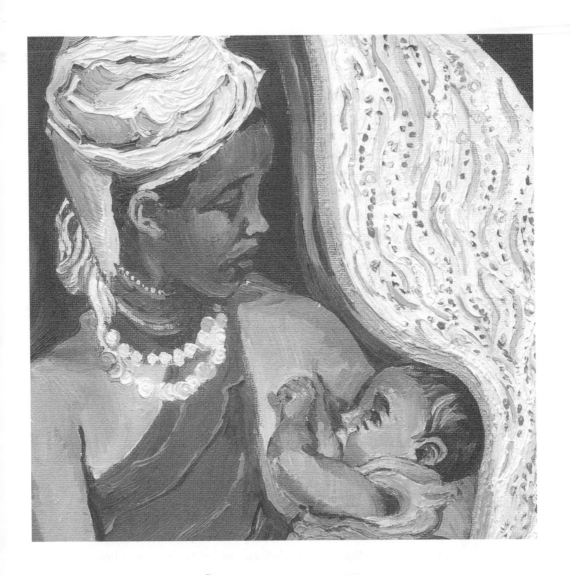

PENTECOST

LIKE FIREWORKS IN THE NIGHT

It was almost too much to take in;
too mind-blowing for them to understand;
too big for human minds to process.
Some said it was like a raging fire.
Others compared it to the unstoppable force of the wind.
Some discovered in it the fulfilment they had longed for.
And there were those for whom it was an explosive
technicolour extravaganza – like fireworks in the night.

But come you did,
and since then nothing has ever been the same.
You have a whole lot to answer for, God-Spirit.
For the result was excitement and unprecedented disturbance
as well as soothing and calming and peace.

But doves don't change lives.
So if we have become apathetic and complacent,
and over-relaxed and easy,
let us understand your presence
as the restless wind of adventure.

Fireworks don't change lives either.
If we have become fascinated by the outward trappings
and impressive rituals, and carefully choreographed formalities
of organised religion, let us understand your presence as fire:
fire that melts and moulds; that reshapes and refines;
that stirs up energy and cuts to the core
and reaches the heart and the centre.

In the quietness now,
we listen to your powerful God-Spirit.
In the quietness now, work your work in us
for our own sake and yours.

A time of reflection

SPIRIT NOW LIVE IN ME

Song: 'O holy dove of God descending ...' (CH4 591), 1st verse

So many people, so many shattered dreams.
For there are those who believed they would be accepted,
but have discovered they are unwelcome and unwanted.
There are those who thought they would be fed,
but whose bellies still gnaw with terrible hunger.
There are those who were promised equal treatment,
but have discovered there are more important agendas to be met.

Great Spirit, listen again to the dreaming of your people.
Mend their hurting, mend the injustice,
mend the unfairness and greed,
and let that happen because you live in me.

Song: 'O holy dove of God descending ...', 2nd verse

There is fear, there is restlessness, there is suspicion,
for change is so often a difficult thing for humanity to embrace.
And yet nothing in this world has ever remained static:
from the beginning of time, the entirety of your intention
has meant that everything and everyone will change.

Spirit, strong as the wind, don't let us put you off.
Keep on pestering us until we are prepared to make changes –
so that the different are included,
the odd ones are accepted,
the 'unlike us' are given equality,
and the feeble given the support that they need.

Great Spirit, listen again to the dreaming of your people
and let the dreams come true because you live in me.

Song: 'O holy dove of God descending ...', 3rd verse

We need to help you to burn more brightly:
to destroy the prejudice that leads to hatred;
to rub out rules that do nothing but denigrate and demean;

to meet the longing of those who pine for recognition;
to support the little people who can't stand up for themselves.

Great Spirit,
you are the answer to all of this world's yearning.
So will you come in power,
and will you come in peace,
and will you take up your living somewhere deep inside of me?

Song: 'O holy dove of God descending ...', 3rd verse, repeated

WHAT DOES THIS THING MEAN?

Voice 1:

'... a noise that sounded *like* a strong wind blowing'. But that's not to say there *was* a strong wind blowing that day. 'They saw what *looked like* tongues of fire.' But that's not to say there *were* flames burning brightly that day. These were the nearest words they could find to describe their strange experience. They had to scramble and feel around to find a way of communicating what they had encountered, for it left them amazed and confused. And so they kept on asking each other: 'What does this thing mean?' But it is little wonder they chose to speak about it in terms of the wind.

Voice 2:

For there's the huge power of the wind:

- strong enough to lift the roofs off houses
- strong enough to capsize ships at sea
- strong enough to blow down trees a hundred feet tall.

Voice 3:

The power of the wind; the power of the Holy Spirit of God in his people:

- causing lives to be turned inside out and upside down
- upsetting long-standing arrangements and traditional habits
- sweeping away deep prejudices and greed and self-centredness, and putting justice and fairness and equality in their place.

Little wonder, when they came face-to-face with the *power* of God that day, they likened it to the power of the wind.

Voice 2:

There's the gradual coaxing of the wind:

- nudging plants so they grow at an awkward angle
- eroding rock-faces until they take on a different shape
- persuading architects to site their buildings where there is less exposure
- causing sailing boats to follow a particular path and specific route.

Voice 3:

The gradual coaxing of the wind; the gradual coaxing of the Holy Spirit of God in his people:

- amending and reshaping individuals, so they do their thinking in a different kind of way
- wearing down what is unhelpful and rough until the face of love is recognised and more obviously seen
- provoking thoughts, and suggesting, and pointing folk heavenwards; until they are convinced a more Christ-like method, a more God-like way, is what's best for the sake of this world.

Little wonder, when they came face-to-face with the *coaxing* of God that day, they likened it to the coaxing of the wind.

Voice 2:

There's the destructive capacity of the wind:

- breaking great suspension bridges in two, in three – and more
- driving flood waters to places they have no business to be
- bringing down aircraft as they make their innocent sky journeys

- smashing up crops until there is nothing left to eat.

Voice 3:

The destructive capacity of the wind; the destructive capacity of the Holy Spirit of God in his people:

- dismantling rigid, brittle opinion and tunnel vision
- rooting out blackness and badness and hate
- demolishing proud ego and self-importance and self-centredness
- crushing arrogance and high-handedness and nasty tongues.

Little wonder, when they came face-to-face with the *destructive capacity* of God that day, they likened it to the destructive capacity of the wind.

Voice 2:

But there's also the creative ability of the wind:

- picking up dandelion seeds, and transporting them so new life can take root
- cooling down atmospheres so living is more possible under a baking, boiling sun
- shifting mountain-loads of sand in the desert to create new contours, and adding variety to planet Earth
- drying up the heavy rains, so crops might grow and flourish, and people can eat, and their bellies are filled, and their hunger is satisfied.

Voice 3:

The creative ability of the wind; the creative ability of the Holy Spirit of God in his people:

- inspiring sacrifice and goodwill and generosity
- planting seeds of compassion and mercy, enabling gentleness to be born again, and willingly shared
- moving mountains of prejudice, so that beauty and tenderness can breathe and thrive
- tidying up the rubbish and debris which exists inside us; washing us clean; making us whole; scrubbing us bright.

Little wonder, when they came face-to-face with the *creative ability* of God that day, they likened it to the creative ability of the wind.

Voice 1:

Amazed and confused, they kept on asking each other: 'What does this thing mean?' Amazed and confused, they could only attempt to find approximate words to explain their encounter with the God-Spirit. And so little wonder they spoke about it in terms of the wind. But little wonder, too, they spoke about it in terms of fire that burns.

Voice 2:

For a fire can be a life-force:

- heat has the capacity to change many things
- warmth sustains and encourages growth
- flames cheer and hearten, their lively movements restore and revive.

Voice 3:

The life-giving fire; the life-giving Holy Spirit of God for his people:

- renewing body and soul and flagging spirit when mood is low
- showing new purpose, providing fresh meaning, establishing cause
- guiding our choice when decisions are difficult, and crossroads confusing
- pointing to the future; establishing hope with the promise of heaven.

Little wonder, when they came face-to-face with the *life-force* of God that day, they likened it to flames of a fire that burns.

Voice 2:

But like the wind, a fire can also destroy:

- solid rocks are melted to liquid
- great forests are scorched, and history turned to ash
- proud structures are demolished, reduced to no more than rubble
- goods gathered disappear, no longer able to be owned and enjoyed.

Voice 3:

The fire that destroys; the paradoxical, destructive force of the Holy Spirit of God for his people:

- melting, moulding, transforming stony hearts, until graciousness and gentleness becomes the new response

- old ways of living wiped out, vaporised, leaving space for new ways to be born
- evil systems and wicked regimes suffocated and starved of oxygen, enabling nobler methods and higher values to have their chance.

Little wonder then that, when they came face-to-face with the *terrible destructive force* of God that day, they likened it to a fire that fiercely burns.

Voice 2:

But a fire that burns gives light:

- a beacon on a hilltop
- a torch to light a path
- a candle-flame that stands as a symbol
- a brightness when all around is cold and dark.

Voice 3:

The light-producing fire; the light-producing Holy Spirit of God, in and for his people:

- indicating the good way through the maze and the mess that living can be
- burning brightly, like an eternal flame amid hopelessness and despair
- signifying Godness as an ever-present option and possibility
- demonstrating divinity above a stubborn humanity which relies on itself.

Little wonder, when they came face-to-face with the *light of God* that day, they likened it to the light of a fire that burns and burns.

Voice 1:

Amazed and confused, they kept on asking: 'What does it mean?' They did well to speak about God in terms of wind. For the power and the coaxing and the creating of that Pentecostal Spirit is very well-known to folk like you and me.

Do you not remember a time in the history of your own experience:

- when you were forced into overcoming your own tight and traditional prejudice
- when you were coaxed into becoming generous, while your instinct was to have and to hold and keep for yourself
- when self-centredness and ego was dismantled and deflated
- when the spirit of creation fanned within you the gentle seeds of compassion, and love was reborn, and beauty and truth could breathe again?

And they did well to speak about God in terms of fire. For is the life-giving, life-changing, light-providing force of that Pentecostal Spirit not very well-known to folk like you and me?

Do you not remember a time in the history of your own experience:

- when a sense of God, and a knowledge of what his High Holiness stands for and demands, served to determine the choice that you made
- when your purpose and place in the order of things became clearer, and your depression abated because of a promise and a hope and a certainty that the uncomfortable present is not all there is
- when you were surprised at yourself, because the goodness which had lain dormant and unused within you, no longer deprived of oxygen, was fed and nourished, so that benefit was passed on to others around you and far away?

All of us, every single one of us, whether we know it or not, are affected daily, even now, by this huge force, this great influence of good, which is nothing other than that same Spirit of God they experienced when they gathered together on that very first Pentecost day.

This was not a one-off, never-to-be-repeated event for the benefit of those who happened to be there long ago. The dynamic divine Spirit is utterly and absolutely eternal, and is something that can never be destroyed.

- Where does the impulse come from that convinces comfortable people they should put themselves out, and shake a can for charity in the High Street?

- Why does somebody force themselves to get up ridiculously early on a Saturday morning to bake scones for a Christian Aid coffee morning, when all their instinct is telling them: 'Don't be stupid. Have a long lie. You've done more than your share'?
- What compels people to use their time and energy to visit those who are lonely, talk to the isolated, comfort the bereaved? I'm saying it is all the work and influence of the Pentecostal Spirit of the God of heaven.

The questions I am asking, you see, are:

- Where does goodness itself come from?
- How, and by what means, is it so frequently and so obviously released?

Small Pentecosts happen all the time:

- each every bit as dramatic as the first one
- each, in its own way, shaping, breaking, melting, moulding ...
- every one as world-changing as the first one.

And therein lies the answer to their question, when amazed and confused they asked each other: 'What does this thing mean?'

LIFE

A WOMAN'S BREAST

'Where do you stand on a mother
breastfeeding her child in the church?' she asked.
'Some of them are muttering.'
(There had been a baptism with lots of visitors that day.)
'Surely you already know the answer to that,' I replied.

'Is a woman's breast *such* an abomination
in the eyes of its Maker?
Should a hungry infant be denied
the satisfaction it needs and craves for?
Is the sight of human flesh,
and the sound of human sucking,
and the mess of a dirty nappy
so hideously unacceptable
that the God of heaven and earth
puckers his lips and averts his eyes
in disapproval, disgust and distaste?

'Flesh of our flesh and bone of our bone he was:
puking and shitting;
bleeding and needing;
wanting and getting;
his mother breastfeeding
her life-giving love to her child in the form of a liquid.

'When the woman with a permanent period touched him,
did he think he should turn her away?
When a beggar with lice stood before him,
did he turn up his nose at the smell?
When a leper whose fingers had gone,
who had been outcast and shunned for so long,
looked for acceptance so he could belong,
was he rejected, despised and dismissed,
or was he welcomed, embraced and even kissed?
Does the one who once sucked at a breast
avoid dirt, mess and danger?'

BUGGER OFF!

This piece has been toned down. Originally it was titled 'Fuck off!' If what is written here is still too dangerous, then substitute 'Get lost!' or 'Take a hike!', or some phrase of your own choosing. This meditation might follow a New Testament reading which contains one of the scriptural references mentioned.

'Bugger off!' That's what he told them
(or at least the first-century Palestinian equivalent).
'Bugger off!' he said.
And as you might imagine, they were well upset.
But as far as we know, he didn't lose any sleep over it.

This young guy was a radical, a rebel, a rabble-rouser,
and he wasn't much given to mincing his words.
See, he couldn't abide the mellifluous mealy-mouthedness
of those who trotted out pleasing platitudes,
and simpered 'There, there,'
as they served up their sympathy like sweet and milky tea.
'Bugger off!' he told them.

He said it to the crowd of pious persecutors who picked up rocks,
intent on using them to pummel a woman to death.
'Bugger off! Leave her alone, unless you have always been pure and pristine yourself.'
And they did: all of them walked away.

He said it to his own alter ego
when he wrestled with some internal, silver-tongued devil
who dangled the carrot of an attractive, but utterly false, way to live.
'Bugger off!' he said. 'I'm taking a different road.'
And he did.

He shouted it at those who grumbled and girned
about one of his most ardent fans:
a woman by the name of Mary,
whose belief in him was such,
whose respect for him was such,
whose feelings for him were such,
that she spent her hard-earned coinage
to practise what *he* preached about generosity.

She emptied a perfume jar all over his feet
to show how much she loved him;
to let him know he was valued and wanted.
She did it to make him feel good about himself.
'What right has she to squander like this?' they complained.
'Bugger off!' And he said it in no uncertain manner.

He said it to the holy thought-police too.
'Why have you not washed your hands before eating
when you know that's what the rules clearly demand?'
'Why have you deliberately infected yourself
when you know exactly who you may and may not touch?'
'Why are you rubbing shoulders with criminals and prostitutes
when you are aware God always prefers those of respectable class?'
'Why do you align yourself with low-lifes and riff-raff
when the scriptures say you must keep yourself squeaky-clean?'
'Bugger off!' he told them.
'It's whether your heart is warm is what matters.'

But there was a gentleness in this man's toughness
and a toughness in the gentleness of his love.
An unusual individual; different; on another planet;
wired to the moon;
but then so is the God of heaven and God of earth.

'Bugger off!' he told them repeatedly
(or at least the first-century Palestinian equivalent).
I think it would please him
if sometimes we had the courage to say the same.

THE AGE OF INNOCENCE

This reflection could be followed by the song 'Take this moment' (CH4 501). 'Bahookie' is a Scottish word for backside.

Reading: Matthew 18:2–3

At five years old, pink is her favourite colour:
the brighter and more garish the better.
She has a great fondness for stuff that sparkles,

and prefers shoes which allow her to skip.
She loves cutting things, gluing things,
drawing things, painting things,
and then collaging them.
Imagination has always been
one of her most attractive features.

It's hard to find words
to describe the deep internal contentment
– a visceral satisfaction really –
of holding, close in cuddle, her little lithesome body:
warm skin, tight, unblemished and smooth;
fresh from the bath, and smelling of apple;
snuggling up in warm woolly dressing gown
(pink, of course!).

And then the predictable, expectant request
(a long-established nightly custom):
'Grandad! Time to magic a bedtime book
from under the cushion!'
(with the help of Daphne the dog).

The ritual search takes place. Nothing there!
And so the magic mantra is recited:

> *'Daphne's bahookie, we've all had a look.*
> *Daphne's bahookie, please magic a book.'*

The little blotting-paper mind, thirsty for information,
absorbing knowledge by the gallon,
wants to know about volcanic eruptions,
ancient Romans and Tyrannosaurus rex.

In childlike innocence,
she believes the best,
sees the best,
looks for the best,
hopes the best,
expects the best in people;
in the world around her;
in all her encounters and experiences.

She lives each day as it comes;
takes people as they are;
accepts what she senses at simple face value.
Her attention is focussed on the moment –
and she marvels at this world in which she lives.

As yet, her thinking largely untainted, unbiased;
her mind uncorrupted, undefiled;
her nature still sweet and wonderfully unfettered.

And so to bed,
to sleep the sleep of innocence;
to dream the dreams of who knows what,
and where, and why ...

And then I look at myself, and think:
Where has my innocence gone?
Dented, bruised and heavily tainted
by a long lifetime of living:
suspicious, distrusting, defensive, often scheming;
guarded and measured in my generosity;
typically thinking the worst ...

Jesus, now I understand why you said it:
Unless you become like a little child,
and take on board all and everything this implies,
you have no chance of starting your living all over again,
and even less of knowing what God's kingdom is
and what it really means.

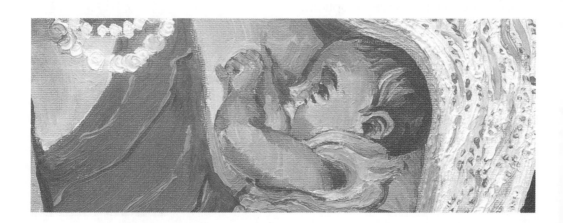

LIGHT IN CREATION'S DARK

Voice 1:

Yours the light in creation's dark,
separating order from chaos,
bringing brightness to the barrenness of what once was.
And then in Jesus, human flesh articulates your way,
for in him renewal finds meaning,
transformation finds focus,
the power of Love is unleashed on the world
and in the people you love.

Voice 2:

You have made your folk
and placed goodness in their hearts –
not so that it can remain there impotent and unemployed,
but be released and set free and put to work
to overcome what demeans and diminishes.
So then, summon out this great energy within us,
for love lies latent.
Do not let our potential remain silent,
nor our Godness remain dormant and unfulfilled.

Voice 3:

We know of the dark forces that stalk the world in our time:
the potency of poverty;
the evil of famine and deprivation;
the power of greed;
the hideousness of war;
the fascinations that distract and serve to defocus us.
Word of the Father, save us from these,
and use us to show yourself to others
so that we ourselves become your life-giving transforming Word.

Voice 1:

In the pain of these hate-filled days;
in the anger that calls for revenge;
in the fear and suspicion that wrecks our relationships;

let our involvement, like the involvement of Jesus,
bring hope and radical change where they need to be.

Voice 2:

Trinity of Love,
draw us into your community of love.
Make the ordinary special,
the unremarkable sacred,
the everyday different and holy,
and so, and therefore, divine.

Voice 3:

Make us, then, more than a group
that happens to hold some things in common;
more than neighbours who nod to each other in the passing
and smile the smiles of polite and respectable convention.
Make your church a community of friendly companions,
and let us be the tasty wine which enlivens experience
so that our own and other folk's living
is richer and far more complete.

YOU SHOWED US HOW TO DO IT

Voice 1:

When this world was flat,
and devils made living a misery;
when exclusion from community was the only remedy,
and isolation and prevention of contact the only cure,
you showed us how to do it.

For you ignored the accepted protocol and propriety
and reached out and touched the untouchable ones,
and encouraged and enabled the different ones,
so that unhappy souls could smile again,
and troubled minds could at last be at peace.
You showed us how to do it,
for where there was generosity and mercy and love,
you yourself were there.

Song: 'Ubi caritas' (CH4 801)

Voice 2:

And still you show us how to do it
by making us angry when we see
little people being treated unfairly,
by making us stupidly generous
when we hear of those who have nothing to eat,
by disturbing us when we are confronted
by injustice and inequality,
by making our hearts soft, and filling us with pity
when we witness humanity hurting its own.
Where there is generosity and mercy and love,
you yourself are there.

Song: 'Ubi caritas'

Voice 1:

Where terrible news about health has been broken,
let your compassion be real.

Voice 2:

Where minds are tormented and restless,
let your peace be real.

Voice 1:

Where modern-day demons and devils
work their hellish work
and reduce and incapacitate and disable,
let your healing be real.

Voice 2:

And in your great power, do all that,
through the love of heaven
which resides in your people on earth.
For where there is generosity and mercy and love,
you yourself are there.

Song: 'Ubi caritas'

THE FACE OF GOD

Voice 1:

Longing God, waiting patiently for us,
and then entering into our experience
when we enter into yours,
establishing a deeper and more intimate relationship
when we are ready to be honest with you.

In this time of stillness now,
as I take time to think about who I am
and where I am
at this particular point in my life,
I meet you in my mind's eye.
I form an image of what you look like
and see the features of your face.

(Pause)

Voice 2:

Perhaps yours is a vulnerable face: weak and fearful;
unsure and scared of what the future will bring.
If so, you understand me,
for over and again you say:
'It's all right. I am here.
I will always walk with you.'

(Pause)

Voice 3:

Perhaps yours is a smiling face: keen to laugh
when I tell you about what has made me happy
and what has given me pleasure.
If so, then you affirm me,
and say you want to be in my company in good times
as well as bad.

(Pause)

Voice 1:

Perhaps yours is a disappointed face,
because you expected better of me.
I know I have let myself and others down.
But your mouth expresses no resentment,
no recrimination, no judgemental disapproval.
Instead your eyes speak volumes
and radiate your passionate encouragement,
and urge me to be more the person I can be.

(Pause)

Voice 2:

Perhaps yours is an angry face,
for despite your hardest work,
despite your best attempts
your people have not learned
and still refuse to listen.

All the grasping and all the suffering;
all the selfishness and all the hunger;
all the self-interest and all the injustice;
all the barriers and all the marginalisation;
it wounds you greatly;
it makes you outraged;
it makes you cry.

(Pause)

Voice 3:

Longing God, waiting patiently for us,
and then entering into our experience
when we enter into yours;
establishing a deeper and more intimate relationship with us
when we are ready to be honest with you,
let us sense you close to us now:
in our thinking, in our dreaming
and in our own dis-ease.

Time for reflection

Voice 1:

God of each and all,
generous beyond measure to each and all,
you know who we are,
you know what we are like.
Look kindly on us.
Deal gently with us.
Help us transform our thoughts into actions,
our intentions into doing and being,
for the future, which is always yours, cradles fresh new hope,
and the future, which is always ours, is the gift of heaven.

O LORD, HEAR MY PRAYER

Voice 1:

You ask us to be your agents in the world, and so we pray now for those who are in difficulty and need to know your love and concern for them at this time.

Voice 2:

God, it's my son. He's mixing with a bad crowd, and I think he's taking drugs. There's no talking to him: he simply refuses to listen to me. I'm at my wits' end and don't know what to do. Lord, hear my prayer as I pray for parents like me who worry about their children.

Chant: 'O Lord, hear my prayer' (Taizé)

Voice 3:

God, my wife has left me for another man. I had no idea this was going on. I still love her but now my life has crumbled. And how can I explain this to the children? Lord, hear my prayer as I pray for people like me who have been badly let down and betrayed.

Chant: 'O Lord, hear my prayer'

Voice 4:

God, what can I do? We're up to our eyes in debt, and the writing's on the wall. On top of everything else, it looks as if I'm going to lose my job. If we have to give up this house, where will we go? Lord, hear my prayer as I pray for folk like me who are sick with worry.

Chant: 'O Lord, hear my prayer'

Voice 5:

God, why has this happened to me? I'm only 52, and they've told me I only have months left to live. I feel it's just not fair! I have done nothing to deserve this. Who else can I turn to now but you? Lord, hear my prayer as I pray for those like me who are filled with fear.

Chant: 'O Lord, hear my prayer'

Voice 6:

God, I'm cold and my belly hurts. I never have enough to eat. Others in this world have so much but I've been born into a life of hardship and poverty. Why have I been given such a raw deal? Will you not feed me? Will you not make me warm again? Lord, hear my prayer as I pray for those like me for whom nobody seems to care.

Chant: 'O Lord, hear my prayer'

Voice 1:

Giving God, you know the hurts of your people. You know by name the worried, the betrayed, the dying, the hungry ... Listen to the cries of all your needy people today, and use us to fill their need and heal their brokenness, because their hurts are your hurts, and their prayers are your prayers too. Lord, hear the prayers of us all.

Chant: 'O Lord, hear my prayer'

WE ARE YOUR HANDS AND FEET

Song: 'For the world and all its people' (CH4 262), 1st verse

Voice 1:

It is hard to keep on following you, Jesus Christ.
It is difficult to be faithful,
for you have this annoying habit
of stopping in all the wrong places,
all the distasteful places,
all the awkward and bothersome places where I would rather not be.
But I know it is the powerless who capture your interest;
and the hungry who are closest to your heart.

Song: 'For the world and all its people', 2nd verse

Voice 2:

Where dirt and danger are present,
you are right there too.
Where selfishness and greed make a mess of things,
you are in the middle of it,
pleading for compassion and mercy.
Where poverty and desperation
give birth to even more misery,
you are there, suffering with your people,
experiencing the ache and the pain of hunger
and the worry and the fear of having next to nothing.

Song: 'For the world and all its people', 3rd verse

Voice 1:

And when we, who are strong,
go with you to those places we would rather not be;
when we stir ourselves from apathy,
and make the effort to shout 'No!';
when we respond to the impulse to demand 'Why?'
and have the courage to protest 'This is simply not fair!';
then there is where the love of heaven is seen
in all its wonderful compassion.

Song: 'For the world and all its people', 4th verse

Voice 2:

You gave us a vision of your kingdom.
You have spoken about
a mustard seed growing into decency and fairness;
salt bringing out the true flavour of what living means;
yeast that stands for truth which conquers evil;
love which transforms earth's people and points them to heaven.

Voice 1:

We are your hands and feet in the world now.
May we hold to these visions of your kingdom,
and do what we can to realise your great dream.

Song: 'For the world and all its people', 5th verse

THE PLANETS SPIN

The planets spin:
their unrelenting rhythm a reminder
of your generous constancy and care.
The seasons change and colours are transformed,
their technicolour a testimony
to your artistry and inventiveness and design.
The sun works to ripen.
The rain works to nourish.
The earth yields its fruit to feed.
You have thought of everything, Provider God,
to make our living full and contented and complete.

This world, and the way it works to sustain us;
these people, and the way they are channels of your love
which touches us;
the permanence of your presence;
the reality of your being;
and all for me, and all from you,
our mother, our father, our lover, our very best friend.

But there is disrespect for the beauty you have made,
for nature is being distorted,
its careful balances upset and disturbed.

The earth is parched, the rain is poison,
the land prevented from giving as it should.

From our self-centred demanding release us.
From our callous carelessness set us free.
From our destructiveness save and redeem us.
Make us long to exist in harmony
with all and everything you have made.

When we lift our eyes,
and look to the hills and all creation;
when we lower our eyes,
and look within ourselves;
when we open our eyes,
and notice the folk who live beside us;
let us acknowledge your signs of love there,
since our home is your home,
on this earth and here in our hearts, incarnate God.

THE HAMPER OF CREATION

When you made the hamper of creation
and filled it with your love,
you intended there to be enough for all:
enough space for all, enough food for all,
enough justice for all, enough security for all;
and that always each should have
their rightful place beneath the sun.

But we know not all are prepared
to be careful and wise with their demands.
And so the hunger of many,
and the poverty of many
because of the callous wastefulness of many,
and the unnecessary deprivation and hardship
we store up for our children and our children's children.

Teach us to treat this world as our friend
as it keeps us alive and supports us,
sustains our living and makes good our days.
Help us to realise it is just plain and downright stupid
to bite the very hand that feeds us,
and gather and gather for now
as if there were no tomorrow to be lived.

May we make good choices,
rooted in the solid rock and sure foundation
of your sensible and crucial Word of Life,
and not the shifting sands of selfishness.

God, hear the cries of this broken earth
and its broken people.
Listen to these cries,
and in your mercy, heal and mend.

IN THE NAME OF LOVE

In the cradle of the womb you are with all,
in the episodes of life you are beside all,
in the composition that is time
you will always be present,
indestructible, universal Love.

We pray for the world and its people.
Some are stuck where they are
and have given up hope of moving on:
from having nothing to having enough,
from hunger to fullness,
from sickness to health,
from distress to peace.
We think of who they may be,
and whether, in the name of Love,
we should go to them.

A time of silence

Some could move but refuse to budge:
from power to humility,
from superiority to equality,
from grasping to generosity.
We think of who they may be
and whether, in the name of Love,
we should go to them.

A time of silence

And some, it seems, can never stand still:
unable to find peace within themselves,
restless with worry or agitated by fear,
or fired up with ambition.
We think of who they may be
and whether, in the name of Love,
we should go to them.

A time of silence

YOU HAVE MADE IT CLEAR

You have made it clear that if we want to help
bring about your kingdom in this world
then we can't just sit back and not interfere,
or close our eyes and ears to what's going on.
Part of your demand of us
is that we should be an active and protesting people,
involved in every area of life,
and not only in the respectable and safe places
that are non-threatening to who and what we are.

You want us to speak out like Jesus and the prophets:
shouting out in protest where injustice is imposed
on those with no voice;
stamping our feet where other feet
are bound tightly with chains of oppression;
thumping the table hard where there is little or no concern
for fairness and equal sharing for all.

Give us the courage to do it,
the sense to understand it needs to be done,
and the vision to see that
'we need a Bible in one hand
and a newspaper in the other'.*

And so when we hear about conspiracies of silence
that are content to allow crowns of thorns
to be pressed deeper into the brows
of those who labour for little,
make us want to interfere.

When we hear about those who are prevented from working
because of gender or class or background or accent,
make us want to interfere.

When we hear about those thirsting
not for guns and bullets, but for peace in their lives,
but who in return are given a sponge soaked in sour vinegar,
make us want to interfere.

When we hear the words 'Might is right',
or 'Ignore them, for they're not significant or important',
make us want to interfere.

God, use us: our energies and passions,
until justice flows like a stream,
and righteousness like a river that never runs dry.

* Attributed to Karl Barth

IN THE STILLNESS

The pleasures of this day:
the people who have made us smile;
the places where we have known we surely belonged;
the recreation we needed to make us function well;
the relationships we have enjoyed that make us secure.
These are God's own doing.
In the stillness, tell God how grateful you are ...

(Pause)

The frustrations of this day:
the people who have made us feel uncomfortable;
the places we never wanted to be;
the situations we would rather not have found ourselves in;
the relationships, or the lack of them,
that are giving us cause for concern.
In the stillness, tell God about the matters that occupy your mind ...

(Pause)

The regrets of this and other days:
when you should never have said what you said;
when you could have done more but chose not to;
when you hurt and harmed instead of liking and loving;
when you thought the worst, instead of looking for the best.
And that other secret personal thing
that only you and your God will ever know about.
In the stillness,
acknowledge your honest disappointment and regret.
Confide in God about who and what you really are ...

(Pause)

Be still, and in the stillness hear heaven's voice:

'I am the one who calls you my friend.
I am the one whose love never fails.
I am the one who says: "Follow me."
Be still and know my forgiveness.
Be still and know I will always say: "Begin again."
Be still and find your peace in me.
Be still and find my peace in you.'

(Pause)

The grace, love and peace
of God the Father, Son and Spirit is ours.
Thanks be to God.
We can begin our living once again.

RODGER'S ~~TAIL~~ BRUSH

This is obviously for children (though 'big children' will like it too).

If you're sitting very quietly, and not in any rush,
I'll tell you a lovely story of a fox who has a brush.
The fox's name is Rodger: he is kind and never rough.
He has many good and friendly friends, including Billy Goat Gruff.

Now, Rodger was out playing in the meadow one fine day,
practising a game called 'Chicken Chase', when he heard from far away
the sound of angry voices: people who had fallen out.
He wondered what had happened to make them scream and shout.

Rodger twitched a whisker, and stood there very still.
He closed his eyes, and twirled his ears, and listened hard until
he could hear what they were saying. (It wasn't very nice.)
For a fox can hear with half an ear the sound of melting ice.
He can smell the moon and stars in June, see a spider at a mile.
He can write and read with utmost speed, and play the harp with style.
For you see, a fox is cleverer than any other thing.
He is wiser than the wisest owl. A fox can even sing!

These children had been very naughty. They had broken every rule.
They weren't any credit to _____ Sunday School.
They had all been playing rounders near the playground, on the grass.
Lots of children were in the game, but it was mostly Mrs _____'s class.
What had exactly happened was difficult to say,
but a window had been broken – and the children ran away!
Instead of waiting to explain, and say what had gone wrong,
the silly things took to their heels, and then it wasn't long
before an argument had started: 'Push off!' 'It wasn't me!'
'It's not my fault!' 'He did it!' 'You're for it. Wait and see!'

Rodger listened carefully. Their fighting made him sad.
He knew, in spite of what he heard, they weren't really bad.
Now Rodger was the children's friend, and they all loved him too.
So off he went as quick as poss' to see what he could do.
When Rodger came upon the scene the kids let out a yelp.
They jumped for joy, and cried: 'Look here! It's Rodger come to help!'
So down they sat upon the grass with Rodger in the middle.
He told them of a thing that happened to him when he was little.

'I was a baby fox: a cub. My favourite food was chicken.
I took one from the farmer's field, and he told my mum – the vixen.
My mother asked: "Now, Rodger dear, please tell me, is it true
that you have taken something which did not belong to you?"

'"It wasn't me!" I told her. But she knew that was a lie.
A clever wise old fox like her could see it in my eye.
"O well, my little cub," she said, "if that's the case, all right.
For you shall have your chicken, dear, at morning, noon and night."

'From then on, all I got to eat at each and every meal
was chicken, chicken, chicken, until I began to feel
that stealing chickens was bad enough, and certainly not wise,
but I'd made the situation worse by telling my mum lies.

'I knew at last I'd have to say: "I'm sorry it's taken so long
for me to own up to the fact that I've been in the wrong."
But at last I plucked up courage, and said "Sorry" to my mum.
She said: "Well, it's OK now, my foxy little son.
For sometimes these things happen to a child, or to a cub.
But don't tell lies about it, for it's difficult to love
a person that you cannot trust; who tells lies as a habit.
Now, what would you like for your tea? A lovely, tasty rabbit?"'

When Rodger finished speaking, there was silence all around.
For every child was quiet with their eyes fixed on the ground.
The children thought, and thought again. They knew what Rodger meant.
They had been daft to run away. After all, it was an accident.

At last one spoke: 'We'll all own up,' he said, 'and apologise.
We'll say we're sorry. We really are! We won't tell any lies.'
'Yes! That's the thing that you must do!' said Rodger with a smile.
He thought: *These kids are really smart!* 'I'll see you in a while!'
'Goodbye, dear Rodge!' the children cried. 'We really have to say
that once again a clever fox like you has saved the day!'

The moral of this tale is clear: if chickens cross your mind,
or if you're tempted to tell lies, then perhaps you will find
it helpful to remember Rodge, that clever little creature
who loves the children in this church, but specially loves the preacher.

A LITANY OF TIME

Voice 1:

Everything that happens in this world happens at the time God chooses. God sets the time for birth, and he sets the time for death.

Voice 2:

We pray for those who have all their life before them, and we pray for those who know their life is soon to end.

Voice 1:

A time for planting, and a time for pulling up.

Voice 2:

We pray for farmers working hard to bring good harvests that will feed the hungry, and we pray for those who destroy the forests and change the balance of this delicate earth.

Voice 1:

A time for killing, and a time for healing.

Voice 2:

We pray for soldiers who are ordered to pull a trigger, and we pray for nurses who do the dirtiest kind of work on others' behalf.

Voice 1:

A time for tearing down, and a time for building up.

Voice 2:

We pray for diplomats who work to dismantle barriers, and we pray for lovers whose relationships are becoming more meaningful and secure.

Voice 1:

A time for sorrow, and a time for joy.

Voice 2:

We pray for those whose hearts we know are breaking, and we pray for those whose news is good, and for whom living is exciting.

Voice 1:

A time for mourning, and a time for dancing.

Voice 2:

We pray for parents who face the prospect of burying their precious children, and we pray for children who lead their parents in a painful merry dance.

Voice 1:

A time for making love, and a time for not making love.

Voice 2:

We pray for women who have been told their womb will always remain empty, and we pray for men who use their partners like rags.

Voice 1:

A time for finding, and a time for losing.

Voice 2:

We pray for those who were rejected and excluded, but who are now finding acceptance and their place in community, and we pray for those who have lost all hope and view the future with apprehension and fear.

Voice 1:

A time for saving, and a time for throwing away.

Voice 2:

We pray for those whose lives are ruined because their finances have crumbled, and we pray for those who are dismissed as unimportant because they are seen to have little to offer.

Voice 1:

A time for tearing, and a time for mending.

Voice 2:

We pray for those who keep would-be helpers at a distance and rip up offers of assistance, and we pray for those who refuse to say sorry to repair what they've done.

Voice 1:

A time for silence, and a time for talking.

Voice 2:

We pray for those who dig themselves into holes because they can't keep quiet, and we pray for those whose tongue lands them in trouble because they can't shut up.

Voice 1:

A time for love, and a time for hate.

Voice 2:

We pray for the unloved who must survive on the margins, and we pray for those who nurse resentments which preoccupy their mind.

Voice 1:

A time for war, and a time for peace.

Voice 2:

We pray the time for war will quickly be over, and we pray that peace will be a feature of this earth and a mark of all its people.

Voice 1:

Everything that happens in this world happens at the time God chooses. And God has set the right time for everything there is.
Amen

ONCE UPON A TIME

Voice 1:

Once upon a time there was an income tax collector by the name of Matthew. He probably lied and cheated every bit of the way. Even so, God smiled at him and said: 'My grace is for you.'

Voice 2:

Once upon a time there was a turncoat by the name of Peter, who said: 'I've no idea who this Jesus person is.' Even so, God smiled at him and said: 'My grace is for you.'

Voice 1:

Once upon a time there was a sneak who would have sold his own granny, never mind his best friend, for 30 coins. Even so, God smiled at him and said: 'My grace is for you.'

Voice 2:

Once upon a time there were some bairns who were making a nuisance of themselves, so the grown-ups decided to chase them away. But God smiled at these wee ones and said: 'Children, my grace is for you.'

Voice 1:

Once upon a time there were more than a few hypocritical legal fanatics who had a habit of preaching one thing but practising another. God smiled at them too, and said: 'My grace is for you.'

Voice 2:

Once upon a time there was a young guy who was filthy rotten rich, who could have been more generous if he'd wanted to. God smiled at him and said: 'My grace is for you.'

Voice 1:

Once upon a time there was a woman who slept around. God smiled at her, and said: 'Sister, my grace is for you.'

Voice 3:

- Maybe you've never cheated, like Matthew.

- Maybe you've never disowned a friend, like Peter did.

- Maybe you've never gone running behind somebody's back to get them into trouble, like Judas.

- Maybe you've never devalued anybody, like the disciples who discounted the children when they came to Jesus.

- Maybe you've never taken the moral high ground and made out that you were holier than thou, like the Pharisees.

- Maybe you've never refused to share what you have, like the rich young man.

- Maybe you've never slept around, like the woman they wanted to stone.

Voice 1:

But if you have done any of these things,
even if you have not done any of these things,
then here is the right place to be.
Because it is here, as well as there, that God smiles to each one personally,
and says: 'My dear, there are no conditions.
My grace is always for you.'

Voice 2:

I'd like to invite you to close your eyes now, and be aware of your breathing ... gentle and relaxed ... your chest rising and falling easily and regularly ... and as you breathe you take into your lungs fresh air ... it is what keeps your body alive ... the oxygen in your lungs passes into your bloodstream ... and from there to every cell and tissue in your body ... your body is being fed by the air.

Even if you wanted to ... even if you tried to hold your breath ... you know you wouldn't be able to do that for very long ... eventually you would have to breathe again ... eventually you would be unable to refuse the life-giving air.

God's grace is irresistible ... it is impossible to stop God from loving you ... it is impossible to refuse the grace that God gives you ... with each intake of breath, breathe in God's free grace ... with each intake of breath, breathe in God's unconditional grace ... with each intake of breath, accept the grace of heaven which you simply cannot refuse.

This is a sacred time ... the God of grace is here among us ... feel this grace stilling your anxiety ... soothing your fears ... taking away your guilt ... mending your agitated heart

... calming the restless worry of your mind ... making your human brokenness whole through the intensity of love. This is a sacred time ... now is when God becomes part of us, and we part of him ... as we allow his grace to penetrate to the very depth, and touch the soul of our being.

A time of quiet

Voice 1:

The grace of the Lord Jesus Christ is with us all.

WE ARE HERE FOR YOU

Song: 'Jesu, tawa pano' (CH4 773)

Voice 1:

Jesus, we are here for you,
and you are here for us,
waiting to welcome in the sound and in the silence;
ready to speak through your Word
and in our own personal prayers.

Jesus, we are here for you because of who you are
and what you have done for us.
We are here because you are our God,
and we are your own beloved people.

Song: 'Jesu, tawa pano'

Voice 2:

Accompanying your folk through time,
in thick and thin
always there when we say your name:
healing and comforting,
soothing and blessing,
restoring and repairing,
forgiving and forgetting,
fulfilling and enriching
so that we can be whole.
In all of this, your time is now
and we are here for you.

Song: 'Jesu, tawa pano'

Voice 1:

Hand-holder, hope-filler,
dream-maker, fear-taker,
heart-warmer, grace-giver,
God of heaven, God of earth, make us new.

Carry on your good work with us:
'take from our souls the strain and stress
and let our ordered lives confess
*the beauty of your peace'.**

So make us whole people:
rounded, healthy, complete;
knowing we have a place;
fulfilled in ourselves by the love
which comes from those who love us:
with the love that is of you.

Song: 'Jesu, tawa pano'

* *John Greenleaf Whittier*

LOVE COMES

This works most effectively when the song ('Love is the touch', CH4 115) is sung by a single voice. It is even more dramatic when the soloist is out of sight.

Song:

Love is the touch of intangible joy;
love is the force that no fear can destroy;
love is the goodness we gladly applaud:
God is where love is, for love is of God. *

Voice 1:

Love comes laughing,
bringing joy, bringing lightness, bringing light.
Love comes laughing in the face of fear, saying:
'Listen! There is nothing more powerful than me.'
Love comes laughing when generosity is offered
and where sharing is gratefully received;
where neighbour helps neighbour,
and friendship is honoured in sacrifice.
Love comes laughing, for love lives there,
for God is where love is, for love is of God.

Song:

Love is the lilt in a lingering voice;
love is the hope that can make us rejoice;
love is the cure for the frightened and flawed:
God is where love is, for love is of God.

Voice 2:

Love comes lightly:
in affirming tones which encourage and hearten;
in gentle silences that say clearly: 'I care for you';
in simple acts of kindness that often go unnoticed;
in cuddles of comfort that say: 'I am for you.'
Love comes lightly, for love lives there,
for God is where love is, for love is of God.

Song:

Love is the light in the tunnel of pain;
love is the will to be whole once again;
love is the trust of a friend on the road:
God is where love is, for love is of God.

Voice 1:

Love comes powerfully,
bringing healing, releasing possibility, instilling hope:
when open hands are held out as a sign of reconciliation;
when embracing arms say: 'I'll help you, for this road is hard';
when solidarity with those who are powerless
creates new vision and births a brand-new purpose;
when troubled brows are soothed, and tear-soaked cheeks are dried,
and worries are put to bed.
Love comes powerfully, for love lives there,
for God is where love is, for love is of God.

Song:

Love is the Maker and Spirit and Son;
love is the kingdom their will has begun;
love is the pathway the saints all have trod:
God is where love is, for love is of God.

Voice 2:

Love divine, living love among us,
give us the grace to be like you.
You have shown us how and why and where.
May we follow you in the way of the kingdom,
until the kingdom comes fully, and the world is one.

* *'Love is the touch of intangible joy', words by Alison M. Robertson, © Alison M. Robertson.*
Used by permission of Alison M. Robertson. From Church Hymnary: Fourth Edition, *Canter-*
bury Press.

TALKING SNAKES AND HEADLESS CHICKENS

From primeval ignorance and talking snakes
to a chosen race, a valued people;
from dejection and exile and slavery
to a promised and promising land;
from hopelessness to clarity of purpose;
from headless chickens to a secure and grounded position;
God Almighty, you transformed again and again.

And such as this you did
because they chose to buy into your vision;
because they understood your Spirit
as active and alive within themselves.

So will you do some transforming now for us?
For there are snakes here:
snakes who want to convince us
our life experience and human cleverness
are enough to solve every problem.
And there are slave-masters here too,
who want to persuade us we are truly captive creatures,
and that your church's future, in whatever form it takes,
is doomed and dead.

And there are headless chickens here as well.
They say we must always be active, never at rest
and never stop to consider what, if anything, we are achieving.

And there are other ones too,
who girn and groan, and say it's not worth the bother,
and wring their hands and whinge and whine,
and protest: 'There is nothing to be done.'

God, like those folk of olden days,
will you help us to invest in your Spirit's ever-present power,
so we can deal with the snakes,
and remove the slave-drivers,
and wring the necks of the chickens,
and so remove them from our thinking and our believing;
so we can set ourselves free
of our own restrictions and free of our tentative selves?

And lest we are arrogant enough
to think that the future of your Body on earth,
your holy, sacred and precious Church,
depends on us, and what we should do to preserve it,
keep on reminding us that
who you are and what you mean
is bigger and greater and far more powerful
than even the best-laid schemes of mice and women and men.

WHEN FINGERNAILS ARE BROKEN

Song: 'Ubi caritas' (CH4 801)

Voice 1:

When fingernails are broken in hard, hard labour;
when the sweat of work is wiped from weary, worried brows;
when skin is damaged, and backs are aching, yet reward is meagre:
God of the rich, God of the poor, you are there.

Song: 'Ubi caritas'

Voice 2:

Where strangers are made welcome,
and where foreigners are friends, you are there.
Where the different are accepted,
and where wee ones are made important, you are there.
God of young, God of old, you are there.

Song: 'Ubi caritas'

Voice 3:

God, make us a flexible people;
open to amendment where it's needed;
willing to spring-clean ourselves and what we do;
prepared to put ourselves out
so that others can get nearer to you;
ready to do what it takes,

though the thought is awkward and unattractive.
For where there is empathy and understanding
of other's needs,
God of the church, God of the world, you are there.

Song: 'Ubi caritas'

Voice 1:

We pray for children
who have been misused and treated as worthless.
We pray for little people
who are denied their rights and whose voice is never heard.
We pray for the poor,
that we may be generous in all our sharing.
We pray for the rich,
that they might be moved by the suffering
and respond as they should.
God, put our hands where our prayers beckon
and transform our passions so they become actions.

Song: 'Ubi caritas'

Voice 2:

We pray in the name of Jesus,
for his sake;
for our own sake;
for the sake of this hurting and unequal world.

INTERNATIONAL DISASTER: A REFLECTION

Reading: John 21:1–14

Do you see how God is working there? Can you see his preferred method of operation? And do you see how effectively he responds when they are at their lowest ebb and have reached the point of worst despair?

- In the face of this monumental physical and psychological disaster, God doesn't offer them holy words and pious platitudes. He doesn't get all religious on them, and tell them to go to church, or to get down on their knees and pray. Instead he responds to their immediate, basic, practical need. They were hungry, so it's: 'Throw your net out on the other side of the boat, then you'll catch some.' His response is as simple – and as useful – as that.

- In the face of their immediate dilemma (hunger, homelessness, aimlessness, zero income, shock) God meets their needs by rolling up his sleeves and getting his hands dirty, and he kindles a cooking fire. He's even gone so far as to think about providing bread to accompany the fish.

This is God-realism; God-activity; God-mending; God-compassion. This is the work of God-love for his people: but it is God-love from below – not remote and distant and high above. And this is how he encourages, and repairs the brokenness; how he restores hope and creates new life in the aftermath of death and devastation and disaster. It is in the most practical, basic, elementary ways that the God of earth reaches out his hands to care for body; to care for mind; to care for soul.

And this is not atypical by any means. Think of all the other times when Jesus met with people who were at the end of their tether, or found themselves in the midst of catastrophe. And think of how his response was always practical:

- he fed 5000 hungry people

- he got his hands dirty by touching, when touching wasn't allowed, and so healed their dreadful diseases

- he used his own spit to repair individual disability and brokenness

- he tended to body, and in that way healed mind and soul.

It's all physical stuff: hands-on, chalk-face activity. No pious prayers, no theoretical religiosity, no weak tea and simpering sympathy. Love in action is God's business. Love that's real and true is his first and only concern.

This same God-love in action can be seen very clearly when, following national or international disaster, so many people respond to devastating events to provide food and shelter and medicine and clothing and all the other essentials people need in order to survive. And is all of that not evidence (if evidence is needed) that God-love was not extinguished on a cross, but lives, and lives again, and continues to operate in and through the hearts of people like you and me, and millions of others like us who have been moved to compassion to care for those who are affected so badly? And is this living love not precisely who and what God is: God alive, God healthy in our world today?

- 'God is love' says our scriptures, not some entity who inhabits the ether like some kind of ghost.

- 'God is a Spirit' says our scriptures, not some old man with a white beard who sits distant and high up on a heavenly cloud.

- 'God is the Spirit of love' says our scriptures, who lives and breathes in his people.

- God is Love itself, Love with a capital 'L'; and there is nothing or no one more powerful who exists on the face of the whole wide earth.

God died on a cross, it's true, but that was not the end of it. There was, of course, no physical resuscitation of a decaying corpse, no revivification of necrosed tissue. But there was spiritual resurrection: the Spirit of Love whom we call our God who lives today.

Resurrection is true. *'Christ is alive! Let Christians sing. The cross stands empty to the sky. Let streets and homes with praises ring. Love, drowned in death, shall never die.'* * Not while you and I and others like us are moved by heaven to respond to disaster on earth.

* Brian Wren, from the hymn 'Christ is alive! Let Christians sing', Brian Wren, Hope Publishing 1969, 1995

LET ALL CREATION DANCE

All your creation dances in rhythm
and you have left your signature there for all to see:
in the ceaseless circling of the planets;
in the nights that relentlessly turn into day;
in the rain that makes a drumbeat on the snowdrop;
in the throbbing of a wasp's flight and bumblebee's wing.
In the rhythm of a dancing creation we sense you,
and glimpse something of the great composer
who invented this great symphony of which we are a part:
your intention to satisfy our souls.

Your people dance lightly in the melody of their living,
and you have left your signature there for all to see:
when fresh experiences make us realise that life is good;
when a lover's heart beats quicker as love is returned;
when hands held out in forgiveness
restore our faith in those who surround us;
when acceptance and care demonstrate clearly
that your love is lively and real.
In the ever-unfolding melody
that is our earthly living we sense you,
and glimpse something of the mind of the One
whose whole composition is meant to satisfy our deepest needs.

And your people dance together in harmony too,
and you have left your signature there for all to see:
as old barriers of separation are dismantled;
as new differences are acknowledged graciously;
as trust and openness are allowed to raise their heads above the parapet,
and unity and togetherness are seen as an important cause.
In the harmony that is our being we sense you,
and grasp something of the will of the One who wants her people
to live side by side in contentedness and peace.

God, help us not to spoil your great invention;
not to upset the regularity of the rhythm,
or put in syncopations that shouldn't be there;
not to make awkward leaps and steps

and so ruin the sweetness of the pleasant and easy melody;
not to augment or diminish the delicate balance
of the work of your hands.
Let there be consonance where there is dissonance,
and give us grace and trust
so that we can sing from the same hymn sheet when we need to,
and so ensure all your children have a place in the choir.

A MOTHER LOOKS BACK

In this liturgy, appropriate slides of classical and contemporary art depicting events in the lives of Jesus and Mary are projected onto a screen, as reflective music is played gently in the background. A different slide is projected for each section. Search the Internet for copies of paintings (e.g. Salvador Dali's St John of the Cross, *which is used near the end of the liturgy).*

Introduction

They say that when you are about to die, the whole of your life flashes before you. If that is true, then for some – those who have lived for long – it must happen at a very great speed: so many memories; so many experiences to recall. But for the one we call Jesus of Nazareth, who did not live for very long at all, there would have been far fewer memories to flash through his brain at the point of his death.

Even so, his short life had been very full, very active. It had been a life of adventure and excitement, but that was accompanied by much unpleasantness and unpopularity, and controversy and violence as well. Anyone with half an ounce of sense could see it was on the cards that Jesus was going to die when he did:

- In the first place, he was nothing but a nuisance to the religious establishment: all those crazy ideas about reinterpreting their precious Law; all his outrageous outspokenness in claiming the love of God was for everyone without exception, and not only for those who were pious and 'kept the faith'.

- He was nothing but a nuisance to the political establishment. The common people referred to him as their new leader. They believed that, through him, they would at last get the justice they deserved and would cease to be treated by the powerful as so much rubbish.

- But Jesus was more than just a nuisance to the military establishment, the occupying Roman forces – in fact he was seen as a very real threat. They had seen charismatic leaders like him before: restless revolutionaries who went about creating trouble, deliberately stirring up feelings of resentment and engineering public unrest. From long experience, the Romans knew the best means of defence is attack. The best solution for dealing with would-be heroes was to rub them out, make them disappear, either that or nail them to a cross for everyone to see.

Jesus of Nazareth was nobody's fool. He knew fine well he couldn't get away with doing the kind of things he had been doing, and saying the kind of things he had been saying for the last three years of his life without some kind of drastic action being taken against him. Jesus was nobody's fool. He knew his days were numbered and that his time on this earth was about to end.

We know his story. We have heard it many times before.

We can only speculate about whether his mother, as she looked back on her own life, had those same kind of flashbacks that people talk about – snapshot pictures; mind images replayed – when the time came for her to breathe her last, and move from life to death.

Tonight, in sight and sound, in word and silence, we listen to Mary, the mother of Jesus; the mother of the one whose life was not easy, but then neither was hers ...

The Annunciation

You brought me nothing but sorrow.
Even before you were born,
there was shame, there was embarrassment;
there was rejection, there was always the great disgrace.
I was only a girl but they showed me no pity.
I didn't know what was happening to me,
but still they called me names
and gave me labels I can't bring myself to repeat even now.
Even before you were born
you brought me nothing but grief and sorrow and tears.

The Nativity

Whatever they might tell you, it was no 'silent night'.
Even though you came from heaven to live your life on earth,
your birth was by no means easy.
Still I remember the hard contractions of labour,
and the moaning, and the piercing, searing pain,
and my desperate cries of: 'God, will you not help me?'

There was sweat, and there was blood,
and there were other fluids from my body as well.
Right from the beginning you were difficult and awkward.
To tell the truth, I really thought I was going to die.
But then, when it was over,
I cuddled you; bathed and breast-fed you.
For you were mine,
and love had come,
and I loved you with the whole of my heart.

Madonna and Child

My precious son, my dearest child,
cream of my heart and apple of both my eyes:

What will your future be? I wonder.
What should I hope for you and dream for you?
And what will you expect of me?
What will you make of life and living?
What will you give to the world?
And what, in return, will this cruel world give to you?

Baptism

The angels proclaimed it at your birth:
You come from heaven.
You are from God.
You are 'of God'.

But why then, if God you are,
this baptism; this cleansing;
this washing clean of what is bad inside?
For God can only be that which is good.

Unless ... you mean to demonstrate your solidarity with broken humanity.
Unless ... you mean to show them that heaven is here.
Unless ... in your baptism you are saying you are one with your people.
Unless ... in doing this you reveal God lives on earth.

The adulterous woman

Good God!
You even consorted with the very worst of them:
thieves, tramps, beggars,
swindlers, low-lifes and a quasi prostitute
like this one here.
You practically were a beggar yourself.
Those were the types you attracted and gathered round you.
For these, you always said,
were foremost in the mind of God himself.
You seemed unable to go with the flow.
You deliberately made yourself unpopular
and insulted the good and the godly.
You always felt you had to stand out as different.
You courted disaster from beginning to end.

In the desert

But it wasn't easy. I know that.
It took courage; it took passion;
it took a unique single-mindedness to follow so difficult a path.
It did cost you, didn't it?
It did cost you so much, I know.
For to be so consistently radical is costly.
To stand out from the crowd is never easy.
To wrestle with yourself can be punishment at its hardest.
There is always a cost in saying 'Yes'
to those to whom the world has already said: 'No.'

The Last Supper

Jesus, how could you?
When you knew the end was near,
how could you arrange a night out with friends?
Did you stop to think of family?
Did you stop to think of those who loved you the most?

Had you told me you were going to die,
I would have been there with you –

savouring every precious moment left to us;
caressing you gently with a mother's hands of soothing love.
Jesus, I would have kissed you had I known what you knew.
Why did you not tell your own mother you were about to die?

Ecce homo

'A man of sorrows and acquainted with grief.'
Jesus, how could you do this to me?
For God's sake, I am your own mother.
How could you make such a spectacle of yourself,
and heap more shame on my head?
Could you not have compromised,
even just a little, and saved yourself?

See what they did to you –
and they say you brought it all on yourself.
Jesus, my son, my boy,
did you really have to drive yourself so hard?
Did you really have to engineer your very own death?

The Crucifixion

And so, this is how it had to end.
You have broken my heart this day.
And all of it; and all of it;
and all of it ...... for what?

The dead Christ

And all of it for this?!
Is this really what it was about?
What will they think of you now, Jesus, my son?
What will they say of you now, Jesus, my son?

God knows, you did what you thought was best.
God knows, you loved like nobody else could.
But it seems they didn't want to listen or hear you.
Everything you stood for;
everything you worked for has been rejected and ignored.

Jesus, my son,
are you asking yourself whether all that you were
and all that you did was actually worth it?
Are you asking yourself now
whether it was just a futile and pointless waste of time?

Blank screen, reflective music fades out …

Song: 'When finest aspirations fail', sung solo (*The Courage to Say No*)

(*Project Salvador Dali's* St John of the Cross *onto the screen.*)

Not for nothing

But is it true, what I am hearing?
For some have said they have seen you,
and others say you are not dead, but still alive.
Some are pointing to the work of your spirit,
and others say their lives have been changed;
they insist you are with them and here.
Some say your power is lasting and for ever,
others know your presence which lives in themselves.
Many still gather to worship you,
and meet you when they come together to share a meal.

And when I look back to the then,
and when I look around at the now,
and when I look forward to what yet will be,
can I, your mother, dare to say this:
not for nothing your pain;
not for nothing your struggle;
not for nothing your hardship, your sacrifice;
not for nothing your walking God's sacred way.

Sing, my soul, when hope is sleeping,
sing when faith gives way to fears;
sing to melt the ice of sadness,
making way for joy through tears.

Sing, my soul, when sadness lingers,
sing to dull the sharpest pain;

sing to set the spirit leaping:
healing needs a glad refrain.

Sing, my soul, of Him who shaped me,
let me wander far away,
ran with open arms to greet me,
brought me home again to stay.

Sing, my soul, when light seems darkest,
sing when night refuses rest;
sing though death should mock the future:
What's to come by God is blessed.'*

Congregational song: 'Lord Jesus Christ, shall I stand still?' (*Enemy of Apathy*) (Can be sung to the tune 'Rockingham')

* 'Sing, my soul', Words © the Iona Community, from Enemy of Apathy, *John L. Bell & Graham Maule, 1988*

MOVE AMONG US ALL

Song: 'Spirit of the living God' (CH4 620)

Voice 1:

The freedom to choose;
the ability to be discerning;
the option to respond or do nothing;
the potential to act in so many ways
so we can hold and heal those who live beside us.
You ask us to be gracious enough to receive
in order that we can give, and give more generously.

Song: 'Spirit of the living God'

Voice 2:

We are your hands and feet now,
and even though you no longer walk and talk
and touch and speak,
and even though we no longer can see you,

still your good Spirit lives within each one of us;
still our minds can be changed
by the power of your great love.

Song: 'Spirit of the living God'

Voice 3:

An old man sits alone and lonely: no one cares.
An infant cries tears of hunger and pain.
A mother knows her breasts will remain flat and empty.
A prisoner sees no prospect of justice and subsequent release.
So will you work your work in us,
and, through your Holy Spirit,
perform more miracles today?

Song: 'Spirit of the living God'

Voice 1:

Will you inspire us to go to the bereaved
and help them to laugh again?

Voice 2:

Will you inspire us to stand up and protest
for the sake of the children who can be healed
if only they are given the chance?

Voice 3:

Will you make us willing to let you prune us
so we can better feed the hungry,
better care for the poor,
better set more prisoners free?
And will you release us and set us free from ourselves
so we can bear fresh fruit,
for the sake of the world,
for the sake of ourselves,
for the sake of your Son?

Song: 'Spirit of the living God'

LIVING DANGEROUSLY

You have made it abundantly clear
that you are distinctly unimpressed
if all we are prepared to do is pay easy lip service to you.
For you are a demanding God:
constantly challenging us to be action men and women,
doers as well as thinkers and talkers.
You want us to be outraged
when we hear of inequality and unfairness,
and make a stand when we witness callousness and lack of concern.
You urge us to be activists in your cause
that strives for justice,
which is the birthright of all your people who live on this earth.

When the poor and weak are ignored,
inspire us to fight their corner for them.
When outcasts are despised and discarded,
irritate us until we make sure they are welcomed and accepted.
When the hungry are starving, and paupers are penniless
and the cheated swindled time and time again,
give us the will and the energy and the means to support them.
Give us the determination to persuade others to do the same thing.

Jesus, you walked hand in hand with the underdogs;
you were fed at the tables of those society shunned and rejected;
you knew the friendship and appreciation of the hurting and suffering ones.
They ministered to you;
they gave you dignity and treated you to their love.

So help us to have the grace to recognise that
the weak can make us strong;
the have-nots can enrich the living of those who have.
And may we have the good sense to understand
that sitting in a cosy armchair doing absolutely nothing
is no better than holding pious opinion
from the comfortable position of a respectable church pew.

CHOICES

The pace of this piece should vary to create a sense of drama.

Voice 1:

The vastness of the sky and the teeming of earth's activity.

Voice 2:

The shaping and the forming and the order
from a seething and untidy chaos.

Voice 3:

The light that shines into the deepest darkness,
penetrating the thickest obscurity.

Voice 1:

You did it all,
and took wonderful pleasure in doing it.

Voice 2:

The greening and the growing.

Voice 3:

The colour, the richness, the depth.

Voice 1:

Everything that lives and breathes,

Voice 2:

and swims and crawls and flies,

Voice 3:

and grows and laughs and sighs,

Voice 1:

called into being by you.

(Pause)

Voice 2:

But did you think this whole thing through carefully enough?

Voice 3:

Are you absolutely certain you got it all right?

Voice 1:

When you decided to invent choice and freedom
were you perhaps too generous in giving it away?

Voice 2:

For the oceans are poisoned.

Voice 3:

The rivers are stagnant.

Voice 1:

The land is laid waste.

Voice 2:

What was once fertile is now impotent.

Voice 3:

The air is dangerous and sinister.

Voice 1:

And the sky has a horrible hole in it.

(Pause)

Voice 2:

Do you still think you were wise,
when freedom has resulted in starvation?

Voice 3:

Do you still think you were wise,
when the future is so insecure?

Voice 1:

Do you still think you were wise
in leaving us to our own devices,
when the world you have made
is wasting away?

(Pause)

Voices 1, 2, 3:

God, we are sorry.
We have not used our freedom wisely.
The choices we have made have not been well thought out.

(Pause)

Voice 2:

The grasping and the taking.

Voice 3:

The destroying and the breaking.

Voice 1:

The greed and the risk and the chance.

Voice 2:

In our choosing we're loosing.

Voice 3:

We are spoiling this, your creation.

LOVE THINKS OF A NAME

Left:

Love thinks of a name.
It is a name that you know very well.
Because this person is old,
sometimes he is lonely and forgotten.
He could do with some friendship and company.

Right:

Let Love work in me.

Right:

Love thinks of a name.
It is a name that you know very well.
Because she is different, people talk about her.
Because she is difficult, people avoid her if they can.
She could do with some support and encouragement.

Left:

Let Love work in me.

Left:

Love thinks of a name.
It is a name that you know very well.
Because he believes he has nothing to give,
then he gives nothing.
Because she needs to feel needed,
she does not recognise other folk's needs.
Because they need to be dealt with kindly
they could do with being affirmed or even challenged.

Right:

Let Love work in me.

Right:

Love thinks of a name.

It is a name that you know very well.
More than once, this person has been hurt.
More than once they have known they are wounded.
Sometimes they get angry and rebellious,
and at other times simply go with the flow
when they shouldn't.
Think of a name.
Think of your own name.
For the name of that person is you.

(Pause)

Left:

God, heal our hurting,
our feelings of isolation and sadness.
Let Love keep us warm and secure,
and let our steps always be light and springy.
And because you know my name,
and because we know our own name,
and because we know the names of others who are hurting,

Right:

let Love work in me.
Let Love work in me.
Let Love work in me for the good of this world.

ALL CREATURES GREAT AND SMALL

Voice 1:

Beautiful Birds of Paradise and slithery, slimy slugs;
marmoset monkeys and scorpions
and freakish fish that inhabit the bottom of the sea;
gentle people, nice people, likeable people,
and those who are ruthless, and full of themselves,
and distinctly unpleasant;
and all of them are yours,
and this is how the world has been made and is meant to be.

Voice 2:

All things come together in you:
the rough and the smooth,
the fascinating and the mysterious,
the ordered and the disorganised,
the loveable and the unloved as well.

Voice 1:

The mountains and the rolling waves
stand as witness to your creativity.

Voice 2:

The trees clap their hands in praise.

Voice 1:

The silence of the night shouts out your glory.

Voice 2:

Children reflect your innocence,
and grown-ups, old and young, belong to you too.

Voice 1:

God, look gently on us
if we have failed to treat your creation with dignity;

Voice 2:

if we have used and abused this earth's precious resources;

Voice 1:

if we have been thoughtless and rough
with those who live beside us;

Voice 2:

if we have looked away, and pretended not to notice
when there is suffering far, far away.

(Pause)

Voice 1:

You are a God who gives us unlimited chances and says:
'It's never too late to begin again.'

Voice 2:

So we thank you for your patience and understanding,
and ask you to encourage our potential.

Voice 1:

Release and realise all the promise within us
so we can make our lives healthy and wholesome,
and help to make the living of others more fully complete.

THE WHY, THE HOW AND THE WHEREFORE

Voice 1:

You are the why, the how, the wherefore ...
beyond our most fantastic imagining,
more and far greater than our wildest dreams.

Voice 2:

Great Love, Lover of Life, Liker of Laughter,
you give life to the loved
and new life to the unlovely.
For grace and goodness are yours;
faithfulness and forgiveness are yours;
warmth and welcome are yours;
and all of these, and more, and more
are who you are,
and what you are,
and what you mean.

Voice 1:

Together like this,
you have called us to worship you:
to sing our songs,
and listen to your words,
and celebrate birth and rebirth
and your passion for us, your beloved people.

Voice 2:

And so, Conceiver of new being and fresh becoming,
Birther of all that is good and hopeful and true,
Midwife of the person we each might aspire to be,
deliver us from what we have been,
and let us sense you among us here on this very day.

Voice 1:

Say our names clearly.
Cuddle and embrace us warmly.

Lead us in the dance of life
as we catch your vision
and glimpse your greatness
and celebrate your power.

Voice 2:

Lord of Light,
friend of each and all,
reveal your love in this time and this space,
as we live out your dreams in the rhythm of our lives
so that we can be whole.

THE WHOLE EARTH SINGS

Voice 1:

This whole earth sings to you,
and creation herself stands witness
to your faithfulness, to your graciousness,
to your love.

Voice 2:

The multi-coloured profusion of the flowering:
evidence of your care in delighting us.
The enigma of the birdsong,
the magic of the moonlight,
the brightness of the daylight,
the comfort of our relationships;
our knowledge of our place and pleasure
in the world you have made.

Voice 3:

Yet despite your care,
in our humanity still we can know unhappiness.
In your wisdom, you allow us to risk and to choose;
and in our humanity, so often we make the wrong choices.

And so there are many who live in need,
many whose best friend is called worry,
many who have hang-ups which diminish them,
and some of those 'manys' are here.

Voice 1:

We ask you to make us whole again.
Let those who have come seeking forgiveness
declare it to God in the silence.
Let those whose hearts are full of gratitude
silently say so in the quiet time to come.
Let those who are restless or empty
sense the God-Spirit who resides deep within them.
And let those who are hurting or grieving
appeal to the One who can mend and repair.

Voice 2:

In the silence,
God of mercy, will you listen to us?
In the silence
will you speak the words each needs to hear?

Time of quiet

Voice 3:

God of grace and God of glory,
in our communion with you and with each other,
may we know the strength of the Father,
the friendship of the Son,
and the inspiration of the Spirit:
the Three in One whose other name
is Holy Love.

BIG-HEARTED GOD

Voice 1:

Big-hearted God,
yours the beauty of these autumn days.
The leaves turn rusty and golden
and the grass becomes bedecked with dew
glinting in the watery, winter sun.
Suddenly the air has a nip to it
and growth is once more temporarily suspended.
Fires are kindled, and smoke seen to rise in tidied-up gardens:
the sweet smell a signal that summer is, once again,
being tucked up in bed.

The sights and the sounds of this world,
the smells and the touch of this world –
these are the things we thank you for:
they are a gift; they are a delight;
they make our living richer and fuller.

Voice 2:

Each morning breaks like the first morning,
and birds sing with elation
at the re-creation of each new day.
Evening time brings the cold winter's moon:
a face in the sky to light up the night.
And all the earth, and all the sky,
and all that lies beyond it
stand as witness to your masterful creativity.
All creation shouts out your glory
and nature sings her tuneful song.

Voice 1:

Yet despite the beauty we bathe in –
this breathtaking canvas which surrounds us
whenever and wherever we open our eyes –
your people misbehave.
They disrespect the very gifts made for their pleasure,
for this planet stands under threat.

Voice 2:

Earth is raped mercilessly
and prevented from releasing her bounty.

Voice 1:

Many go without,
while others say 'I must always have more.'

Voice 2:

Nature's balance and creation's provision are used and abused.

Voice 1:

God, forgive the stupidity of it.

Voice 2:

Forgive the greed, the grasping,
the storing up, the lack of generosity.

Voice 1:

Turn us round.

Voice 2:

Make us see sense.

Voice 1:

Make us more careful.

Voice 2:

Give us the wisdom to treat the earth and its people
as most precious things.

Voice 1:

Your kingdom, and not ours, come on the earth.

Voice 2:

Your kingdom come
because your will, and not our own, is the only sensible way.

Voice 1:

Your kingdom come in care and carefulness.

Voice 2:

Your kingdom come – and let it come quickly
for the earth has had enough.

THE WHISPERER

Narrator:

'What I tell you in the dark, utter in the light. What you hear whispered, shout from the housetops.' *(Matthew 10:27)*

Through the years, there's been a lot of talking in the dark. In times of fear and confusion, self-doubt and God-doubt, He whispered quietly into our hearts words we somehow couldn't explain, but neither could we deny them. In times of quiet intimacy He made His presence known, and His spirit lived and breathed in us.

Voice 1:

He whispered softly to him that day, and it is etched in his memory. Well, you never forget that day, do you?: the day you first actually planned and plotted to do something wrong, knowing it was wrong, but intending to do it anyway.

He got away with it though (or so he thought), until the misgivings started: the stomach ache and the awful feeling that he couldn't risk looking anyone in the eye because they'd surely see his guilt. The horrible knowledge that he'd done wrong.

As he struggled with himself and his darkness, the Whisperer came and reassured him he was loved and forgiven. He then found the courage to say he was sorry, to admit to himself and others he'd made a big mistake. And when he did this, the Whisperer smiled and spoke again words he would hear so many times afterwards during his life: 'You are forgiven.'...

Narrator:

'What I tell you in the dark, utter in the light. What you hear whispered, shout from the housetops.'

What then will he say for all the others who struggle with guilt and regrets and misgivings in the dark? How then can his heart be silent when so many other hearts cry out for a second chance, a new beginning, and long to hear these words: 'You are forgiven'? The whispers he heard as a child must not be silenced now, because he has been called to shout from the rooftops that forgiveness and new beginning is what God wishes and prays for us all. These are gifts we can offer each other ... our only way forward. The whispers must not fade into nothing. 'What I tell you in the dark, utter in the light. What you hear whispered, shout from the housetops.'

Voice 2:

He whispered softly to her as she held her beautiful new baby, as she counted fingers and toes and stroked that tiny, perfect face, laughing as it turned towards her touch, already looking for food.

The words she heard in her heart sang out as she looked up at the joyful, astonished disbelief on the face of the one standing beside her: the one whose carbon copy now lay in her arms.

She felt His presence there with them as she realised there was a love at work – love more powerful than anything they could ever hope to achieve on their own. When her heart was bursting to thank someone for the gift she'd been given, the Whisperer accepted with pleasure.

Narrator:

'What I tell you in the dark, utter in the light. What you hear whispered, shout from the housetops.'

What then will she say for all the other babies who are starved of food, of love, of a chance? How can her heart be silent when so many other hearts burst with sorrow when their gift is taken away? The whispers she heard must not be silenced. She has been called to shout from the rooftops that all children are gifts from God to the world: that they have a right to live, to eat, to grow, to be loved. The whispers must not fade into nothing.

Voice 3:

The man told us He'd whispered softly to him as he sat in the waiting room. What an ironically appropriate name for the place: 'The Waiting Room'.

As fear gnawed and loneliness crept in beside him, despite the full chairs all around, he said He'd stayed there with him and entered the loneliness, held a candle to the dark. When the worst news came, the Whisperer stayed there with him just as He'd promised He would, bringing an inexplicable sense of reassurance, a comforting presence. Holding him in the promise that the fear and pain in the present was not the future … It was not the end. When the end came, the Whisperer would take him on to a new beginning where there was no more waiting.

Narrator:

'What I tell you in the dark, utter in the light. What you hear whispered, shout from the housetops.'

What then can this man say for all the others who wait and fear? What comfort can he bring them in their loneliness? How can the words, which brought him comfort and peace, be spoken in the cold light of day?

How can his heart be silent when so many other hearts burst with sorrow and fear as their gift of life is taken away? The whispers he heard must not be silenced because he has been called to speak in the light what he heard in the darkness. The whispers must not fade into nothing. God is with us and will not leave us, in pain, in suffering, in other people's badness.

'What I tell you in the dark, utter in the light. What you hear whispered, shout from the housetops.'

Through the years, there's been a lot of talking in the dark. In times of fear and confusion, self-doubt and God-doubt, He whispered quietly into our hearts words we somehow couldn't explain, but also couldn't deny. In times of quiet intimacy, He made His presence known and His spirit lived and breathed in you and me.

What then will we say for all the others who long and look and strain to hear a whisper? How then can our hearts be silent when there are so many other hearts He longs to touch? The whispers we have heard must not be silenced because we have been called to shout from the rooftops so that all God's children can see light in their dark times, know they are not alone, know they are loved with a love that is much more powerful than anything we could ever hope to achieve on our own.

The whispers must not fade into nothing. 'What He's told you in the dark, utter in the light. What you've heard whispered, shout from the housetops.'

Sally Foster-Fulton

WHAT THE STORY DOESN'T SAY

Readings: Luke 15:1–2, 11–32

Narrator:

'And all the tax collectors and sinners were coming near to him to hear him. The Pharisees and teachers of the Law murmured, saying: "This one receives sinners and eats with them." And he spoke to them this parable' ... Or maybe it would be better if it said: 'He allowed this parable to speak to them.'

The voices from within this story touch and cajole, comfort and challenge. If we listen to them, they can show us ourselves, and that is the power of this story.

This morning, we are going to listen, and we are going to allow this story to speak to us. Listen to it, you Pharisees and teachers of the Law. Hear its words, you sinners and tax collectors. Let it speak to your heart all of you 'somewhere in betweens'.

Younger son:

It says in the Bible story about me, 'He came to himself.' Well, I did, but not when they say I did. At first, I remembered which side my bread was buttered on. I knew where I'd be better off – and it wasn't sitting in pig ... you know what I mean. No, I came to myself when I saw my old man drop his shovel and run across that dry, half-planted field to throw his weary arms around my good-for-nothing neck. That's when I came to myself. That's when I realised – not which side my bread was buttered on – but which side I wanted to be on, what kind of person I wanted to be. It was when I realised it wasn't too late, that I was still loved, that unbelievably, I was forgiven, I could still make a fresh start.

Older son:

It says in the Bible story about me that 'I was angry'. Well, that's a little understated. I was furious! That brother of mine was lost and now he was found, and sitting there, pretty as you please, eating my fatted calf.

You know, there's a little point nobody seems to pick up on – a little point that made a big difference. He'd taken half of what belonged to our father, *before* he was rightly entitled to it. It was still my very-much-alive father's property – property he'd worked hard for and on all his life. He'd taken what was not yet his to take, and from now on, he would be taking what would someday rightfully be mine! Put yourself in my place. How would you feel? Overwhelmed with brotherly love? I don't think so!

You know that a lot of you people secretly identify with me. A lot of you, deep down, agree with my actions. A lot of you would have done exactly what I did. But you would have been wrong too. My brother made a mistake – a big one. He was selfish and greedy. But aren't we all? Don't we all mess up sometimes? Maybe not as spectacularly as my little brother, but look into your own heart? Aren't there some things there that you wouldn't want us to see? Well, the point of my story is that, after a lot of fuming and arguing and learning, I finally saw that about myself. The story in the Bible doesn't tell you this, so I thought I'd come and clear the air.

I suppose I 'came to myself': realised which side I wanted to be on; what kind of person I wanted to be. And I realised too that it's never too late for anybody to make a new start. I realised that I am always loved, unbelievably forgiven. And one more thing (while I'm on a roll): what I really wanted was for my father to love me. That was why I was so angry. But love is something that is limitless: the more you give, the more you have.

Father:

It says in the Bible story about me that I had two sons. A truer word has never been spoken. There have never been two more different children, and we loved each for himself. Everything we had was theirs, but they were always at loggerheads. The older boy – well, he just seemed to know what was right. All we had to do was ask him, or tell him, or sometimes steer him in the right direction and he'd go there. The younger one though – that was a different story. Black was white, day was night, wrong was right. Anytime we attempted to ask him or tell him or even steer him in one direction, he'd head straight for the other. There was only one way that boy would ever learn anything: the hard way.

When he asked for his inheritance we knew it was a risk, but we also knew the only way to keep him was to let him go and find out for himself what side he wanted to be on, what sort of person he wanted to be. When I saw him coming back up that path, my heart just about leapt up into my mouth. Our son was lost, but now he's found, loved, forgiven, saved. We simply had to celebrate!

Well, the older boy has come around now. We knew he would eventually. He just seems to know what's right.

Mother:

It doesn't say anything in the Bible story about me, but I'm the second half of that 'we'. And it doesn't say quite enough in that story about the pain and the sacrifices and the risks love asks you to take. That story only leaves to your imagination the sleepless nights, the worrisome dreams, the heartache of parents who have no idea ... Well, as I said, you can only imagine.

But please hear our story. Hear it as it was meant to be heard because it is about God: the God who will always love you; the God who longs to protect you and shelter you under her wings; the God whose love is so vast that there is no share of an inheritance, and yet more than enough for everyone; the God who calls you to live in that same love by being as generous and forgiving to others as God has been to you. For in this God you will come to yourself. In this God, you will become the kind of person you hoped you'd be.

Sally Foster-Fulton

THE CLOAK

Reading: Mark 10:46b–52

Hands pushed him along. Voices shouted directions. Curious onlookers accidentally got in the way: ancient-day rubberneckers! Among the crowd that shoved him forward were some who had walked right on past him for years as he sat on his cloak begging by the roadside.

He'd never been one to make a fuss: he just sat there and let his situation speak for itself. Most folk would give him something. It was part of their law and custom to give a bit to those who couldn't look after themselves. So people felt obliged and they gave – leftovers and afterthoughts mostly, but at least it was something.

He would survive. A few coins tossed out of duty, the odd meal to keep him from wandering the streets too much and, of course, he had his cloak: someone else's cast-off, but it was his most prized possession. It was, for all intents and purposes, his only possession. And it was important, essential. He needed that cloak. Without it he'd freeze. Folk threw the money he begged on to it. It gave him some cushion as he sat day after day; and it protected him from the sun on days when it was scorching.

He knew it wasn't much of a life, but it was the devil he knew. He knew his place and for the most part he stayed there, didn't make waves, accepted it. But he'd been listening: he always listened to bits of conversation. Gossip that came from all over passed his spot in the road. And he'd heard about this guy, this Jesus of Nazareth. He was fascinated by what he'd heard: that this Jesus talked about the poor being blessed, the mournful seeing God.

Well, he was certainly poor – and he'd settle for seeing anything! Deep down, he began to question his situation. He'd heard rumours that this man was always stopping for the strangest reasons: to hold children; to tell a story that left you with more questions than answers; to eat with no-goods and riff-raff; and then to feed crowds and heal people that most folk wouldn't even speak to. Sitting there, day after day, he began to wonder. Would Jesus of Nazareth stop for him?

And then the day came. It's amazing how these things happen! Right there, near his spot, on his road. The crowd started making noises first. He heard bits of excited conversation: hints and rumours, and then there was a lot more noise, and the name being said. Suddenly, he realised that he couldn't let this chance just slip by: walk right on past as so many others had and did. So he started to make a noise (quite unlike him really). Once he started, he couldn't stop. 'Jesus, son of David ... have mercy on me!' Over and over again he shouted until the crowd got sharp and annoyed.

'Shut up! Don't be a nuisance! Let the man get on to more important things.' But he continued; and suddenly, the tone began to change. Voices urged him to his feet. 'He's calling you. Hurry up!'

This was a turn-up for the books. It was his chance, and he wasn't going to miss it. He even left his cloak. He jumped up, threw it down in the dust, and felt his way through the crowd to the man who'd called for him. He threw down his cloak which was so important, so essential. He needed that cloak. Without it he'd freeze. Folk threw the money he begged on to it. It gave him some cushion as he sat day after day, and it protected him from the sun on days that were scorching. But this was his chance, so he threw it down to grab something else. He left it behind, the cloak, the old life, the devil he knew. It doesn't say that he ever went back for it. It says: 'Immediately ... he followed him along the way.'

(Pause)

What would have happened if he'd gone back for that cloak: just in case; for protection; a little cushion and comfort? What would have happened if he'd wrestled back through the crowd, stooped down, brushed it off, folded it, collected the coins that had scattered as he ran? It would have been such a big temptation. Some would say that it might even have been sensible, advisable ... for protection, as a cushion, as a comfort. But he didn't. It says very specifically (for all Mark's details are there for a purpose): '*Immediately ... he followed him along the way.*'

The tale of the cloak is important, essential. This old story has a lot to tell us today about clinging to things (ideas, traditions, possessions, institutions) for protection, for comfort, as a cushion. It has a lot to say to us today about our very human tendency to revert to old, comfortable, known ways ('the devil we know') when the new way seems daunting. It calls us, as a church, and as individuals, to be willing to leave behind some of the things we think we need so we can follow Christ, the strange itinerant preacher who will inevitably ask you to stop on the way, to hold children, to tell a story that leaves folk with more questions than answers, to eat with no-goods and riff-raff, and then to feed crowds, to heal people that most folk wouldn't even speak to.

You need your hands and your hearts free for a job like that. The leaving of the cloak ... it's a good story.

Sally Foster-Fulton

DEATH AND BEREAVEMENT

OPENING SENTENCES

Listen carefully, you who have come here today.
This is a place where the God of heaven
has often been known to speak to his people.
This is a place where the God of earth
has often been known to comfort his people.
This is a place where, many times in the past,
the pain of grief has been gently soothed;
where hurting hearts have been healed
and made whole again;
where restless thoughts and anxious imaginings
have been calmed and stilled and taken away.

For here is where God's own people
come together in community:
to dry each other's tears of disappointment;
to support those among us who are most unhappy;
to mend the hurt and brokenness
of those who experience the keenest
and the strongest sense of loss.

Here then, is where hope and strength can be found:
in the sincerity of a handshake;
in the warmth of a cuddle;
in the simplicity of a smile;
in the silence of a shared understanding
that needs no words to accompany it.

And all of that speaks loudly
of the love and all-embracing compassion
that comes to earth from heaven itself.

This then is the right place for us today,
for _____ has died.
And for those who were closest to her,
and who loved her the most,
the disappointment runs deep;
and there is much sadness and grief.

But we are here too to express our gratitude.
For on this day of all days,
whatever our faith, or honest lack of it,
there is a part of all of us which senses and knows
it is right and it is good to give thanks
for a life consistently lived in glad celebration;
a life marked by the closest
and most meaningful kinds of relationships;
a life in which so many friendships of depth
were made with folk whom she met along the way.

And we give thanks too
for the privilege that has been ours
of knowing this fine and decent woman;
for the way in which she touched our lives
so that in the process,
our experience was all the richer, all the fuller,
our own living made more wholesome
and more complete.

PRAYER OF THANKSGIVING

God who is love itself,
even in the sadness of this day,
we turn to you with thanksgiving and with hope:
hope that, now _____'s living here is done,
she is now your honoured guest
at the banquet you have prepared
for those who are humble and kindly and good.

We give thanks to you
for the privilege of knowing this fine woman.
We give thanks for the many ways
she gave herself in relationship –
to her children, and her children's children,
and the rest of her family too
who loved her so well in return.

For that special relationship
she and _____ enjoyed together,
and the happy years they shared with each other,
content in one another's company;
secure and confident in their home
that was always such a warm and welcoming place
for all who came there.

For her busyness; her friendliness;
for her easy-going nature,
and her cheery and inoffensive ways;
and for the way she cared for many people
and so made their living easier and better
because of the love and compassion
that was in her heart.

For all of that, and for all the good times
we were able to share with her personally,
and for all _____ will continue to give –
because her influence, her spirit, continues to live
in the hearts of those who love her most –
then thanks be to you.

IS IT SUCH A TERRIBLE DEAL?

I'm 85!
And now they've mentioned the word 'cancer'.
I prefer to call it a growth, a swelling, a tumour.
Yes, I think I'll call it a tumour:
that's gentler, more acceptable, less shocking to say.
Maybe they mean it's benign.
But I'm not asking in case they tell me it's not.
A tumour can sometimes be cured.

Who am I kidding?
My family? My friends? Myself?
A tumour can also be fatal.
I think I'm on my way out.

But is that really so terrible?
Is the long sleep so abhorrent?
Is the prospect of blankness so tragic?
And of course, there's always the prospect
of a bright new shining day.

The truth is I'm tired.
I've had my life. I've done my bit.
One part of me says this:
'I really am ready to go.'

I've always known this is the deal:
you're born, you live, you die,
and then you are forgotten –
maybe not tomorrow,
maybe not next week,
maybe not next year.
But that is the unavoidable, eternal, natural deal.

Is it really such a terrible fate
when all is said and done?
When my visitors arrive later on,
I think I'll tell them I've got cancer.

SHE MADE IT EASY FOR US

She made it easy for us.

'I'm sorry, it's cancer,' the doctor told her.
'It has spread, and there's nothing we can do.'
'I'm 85,' she smiled, nervously.
'What else can I expect?
At least I know I won't be run over,
and my body made a terrible mess of by a 44 bus.'
She made it easy for us.

'What are you feeling?' I asked her,
fully expecting she would say
she was paralysed by fear,

immobilised by terror,
depressed beyond measure,
now that death was firmly on the cards,
and staring her so squarely in the face.

'I'll tell you what I feel.
Death is in the order of things,
and the prospect is neither dread-filled nor abhorrent.
For me, the long sleep is not as unattractive as you might think.
I am tired. I am weary. I've done my living.
I am tired. I am weary. I am ready to go.'
She made it easy for us.

But then these startling words
from one who had been so faithful to her church,
so committed to her God,
who seemed so secure in what she was doing
and in what she believed.
For this was the lady who had never missed a Sunday
and whose faith had always seemed certain and quite beyond question.

'I don't know if there is a God,' she said awkwardly.
'And I'm just not sure that, when I wake up, if I wake up,
there will be a brand-new morning and a bright new day.'
She made it difficult for us.

No! It was the faith she had been taught and told
that was making it difficult for her.

But this wasn't the right moment
to suggest the child-friendly pictures from Sunday school
were no more than helpful, reassuring imagery;
intended to take away fear.
And it wasn't the right time
to say that being welcomed by cherubims,
and smiled at by seraphims,
and serenaded by heavenly choirs
in the throne room of heaven
were no more than pictures to cling to for comfort.

And it definitely wasn't the right place
to suggest she would *not* meet resuscitated corpses
or reincarnations of the folk she had once known.

'I saw a new heaven and a new earth.'
She'd been told she must take all this literally,
but in the face of reality it just wouldn't do.
It wasn't the right moment, the right time, the right place
to suggest a more acceptable and reasonable alternative:
that resurrection of spirit is real;
that the essence of her wholeness can never die;
that something of who and what she is
will continue in her children, and in her children's children,
and so on for ever and ever.

They made it difficult for her.
She made it easy for us.
Her last words on the subject were these:
'Of course, I am hoping that in all of my doubting
I am wide of the mark, well off the beam,
totally and completely wrong.'

She made it easy for us.

REMEMBERING

WORDS FOR REMEMBRANCE SUNDAY (1)

Voice 1:

The world remembers
and today the tears of many will fall.

Voice 2:

Tears of resentment for a life that was stolen,
and the love once given so freely
can never be given again.

Voice 3:

Tears of anger for a life that was stolen,
and the dreams of what might have been
can never be fulfilled.

Voice 1:

Tears of regret for a life that was stolen,
and youth and vitality were halted,
and energy and passion were stilled
and now remain silenced for ever.

Voice 2:

Tears of pride for a life that was given:
in a brave act of sacrifice;
in a courageous deed of compassion;
in a deliberate act of selflessness.

Voice 3:

And so in the remembering,
with resentment, with anger,
with regret and with pride,
are all these tears and all this pain
and all the hurting.

Voice 1:

But for us here, the people of God,
we who have come on this day not only to remember,
but first and foremost to worship the God of peace,
this is also a day for thanksgiving and gratitude.

Voice 2:

But not thanksgiving for victory in battle,
or triumph over those who are also
God's precious children,
nor gratitude for might and force and strength.
This is a day for heartfelt praise and thanks to God
that war and conflict is not the only way;
that God has provided an alternative
to humanity's weak and futile attempts to live as one;
that God's Son Jesus has shown us another way;
that God's own way is the only true way to peace.

Voice 3:

And we are here to pray
that weapons of war are not put to use again;
that terrible inventions of destruction and suffering
are never more activated;
that humanity will listen and hear the voice of heaven which says:
'This is your way.
This is a foolish way.
This way is not mine.'

WORDS FOR REMEMBRANCE SUNDAY (2)

Voice 1:

For some this time is right.
The busyness will cease;
the traffic will be halted;
the noise of the world will become still –
for a time.

Voice 2:

The gentle wind will rustle the drying, dying leaves
until they also fall to the ground in silence
in their own symbolic enactment
of something that happened because of the madness that is war.

Voice 3:

The loss is real – for some.
The grief is raw – for some.
There is a rightness in making this space and taking this time
to remember the face and recall the voice;
to imagine the life which was stolen.
For some, this time is right.

Voice 1:

For some this time is wrong.
The busyness of the world will not cease,
not even for a moment.
For schedules must be fulfilled
and deadlines must be met;
journeys must be completed
and appointments must be kept.
The hurrying world moves on.

Voice 2:

The angry wind tries its hardest
to strip the healthy leaves from the trees.
But the time is not yet.

They remain firm and refuse to fall.
They witness that life must still go on and on.

Voice 3:

The loss means nothing – for some.
The grief is absent – for some.
The memories, there are none – for some.
There is no point to make this space and take this time
to remember a face, to recall a voice,
to imagine a death in anonymity.
For some this time is wrong.

Voice 1:

This earth on which we live – for a time;
its people we love and who then leave us – for a time;
the world remembers them, and then it moves on.

Voice 2:

Or, it moves on without having remembered.

Voice 3:

And the God of the living and the dead
holds the whole thing together in tension.
Heaven's Spirit of unity holds it together
in the precious cradle that we call love.

WORDS FOR REMEMBRANCE SUNDAY (3)

In the silence, from the silence:
the peace of God for those who take time to listen.

In the silence, from the silence:
God's word of calm for those who,
in their remembering, find only distress and regret.

In the silence, from the silence:
God's uncomfortable reproach

for those who, in their remembering,
cannot find it within themselves to forgive.

In the silence, from the silence:
God's smile of affirmation
for those who are surprised to discover
they feel little or nothing at all.

And in the silence and out of the silence,
God's presence to encourage those who,
in their remembering,
know their grief is still very heavy,
and their suffering no less raw to bear.

A powerful, active and happening silence then,
not simply an empty space.
A potentially life-changing silence,
not simply a sterile space.
A gentle silence, a disturbing silence,
now carved out of our living and being.
For here, in the silence, out of the silence,
God makes his peace with the people of Earth.

Let us now stand, if we are able,
or remain seated,
remembering the sacrifice and the suffering,
rejecting the way of war that leads to death,
praising the way of God that leads to real and true living,
praying the world will learn to live in peace with itself.

WORDS FOR REMEMBRANCE SUNDAY (4)

Voice 1:

At the 11th hour, on the 11th day, in the 11th month,
the busy traffic will cease,
and the noisy clamour of the world will be silent
for two short minutes.

Voice 2:

At the 11th hour, on the 11th day, in the 11th month,
cash registers will not ring,
and important and urgent tasks will be put on hold
for two short minutes.

Voice 3:

At the 11th hour, on the 11th day, in the 11th month,
thoughts will turn to long ago,
and for some it will seem like only yesterday.

Voice 4:

But two short minutes can never be enough
to acknowledge the sacrifice,
to fill up the emptiness,
to comfort the pain and the grief,
to teach this warring world there is a much better way.

Voice 1:

At the 11th hour, on the 11th day, in the 11th month,
the traffic will not cease,
the cash registers will continue to ring,
work will carry on as usual,
and thoughts will be of this day's battles, bullets and bombs.

Voice 2:

And in two short minutes
victories will be secured or lost.
For this world has not yet learned its lesson:
it has chosen to refuse to understand
and has been unwilling to embrace
and take on board the road to peace,
the method of love, the better way.

Voice 3:

And folk might be forgiven for believing
the sacrifice was all for nothing,

the emptiness inside has been ignored,
the pain has been passed over as unimportant,
for our world is still at war with itself.

Voice 4:

At the 11th hour, on the 11th day, in the 11th month,
what can we do,
where can we go,
to whom, in our disappointment, might we turn?

Voice 1:

To the God whose other name is Love,
and whose gospel is a gospel that speaks of peace.

Voice 2:

To the One who enters into our deepest grieving,
and offers us refuge,
and is our strength,
and gives life meaning.

THE BOY IN THE STRIPED PYJAMAS*

I was the one who was there.
I was the one who went through it,
but you're only hearing my story here today.

What kind of bloody animals were they anyway?
For God's sake, I was only nine years old after all.
And if you're shocked, or insulted,
or offended by my language,
then to tell you the truth, I really don't care.
For there are worse things
that can happen to you in this life
than to listen to a child when he swears.

What kind of bloody animals were they?
They were fathers of pretty little girls,
mothers' sons, favourite uncles,
doting husbands, family men,

upright and respectable members
of their own communities.

Often they had sat by the fireside
and contentedly watched their own children play.
They had patted babies' backs,
tickled babies' chins,
rocked infants gently;
the kind of men who found their pleasure
in making little ones laugh.

They had looked on with pride
as they watched daughters blossom
and grow into maturity.
They had congratulated sons,
and encouraged them
with an enthusiastic: 'Well done!'
But, my God!
What kind of bloody animals were they?
How could they transform so dramatically?
How could they become such monsters?
How could they change, and become so different,
and turn into such subhuman beasts?

They made us wear flimsy, striped pyjamas,
tattooed numbers on our arms,
and gave us hardly anything to eat.
In freezing temperatures we shook and we shivered.
They made us slaves,
they made us suffer,
they turned us into feral creatures: jungle animals.
And if anyone became sick,
they were taken away
and made to disappear.

For idle amusement of an evening
they would set their dogs on us,
and then laugh.
A baby's arm was ripped open,
an old woman's face removed,
a teenager's leg lacerated from groin to knee.

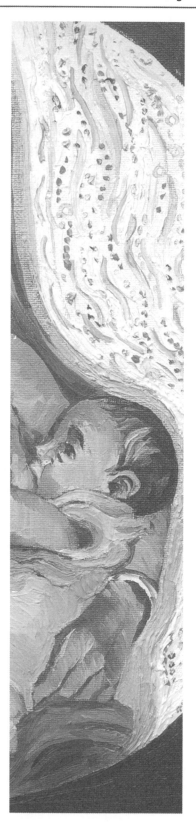

You've no idea the damage that can be done
by snarling, vicious teeth.

And then, just for the fun of it,
the lashings and the beatings.
No excuse needed:
a soldier's amusement,
a jailer's prerogative:
another prisoner dead.

Thick black smoke rose daily.
There was nowhere to escape;
nowhere to avoid the sickening stench
and the nauseating smell.
It clung in the air,
it lived in your nostrils,
it always was with you.
We knew what was happening;
we knew what it meant ...

What kind of bloody animals were they anyway?
I've thought about it a lot,
but can't come up with an answer.
I was only nine years old after all.
But one thing I do know for certain:
once upon a time those men were ordinary folk.
Maybe they just got corrupted by the fact of war;
got caught up in the purest kind of evil
that war always breeds.

And if you're shocked, or insulted,
or offended by my language,
then to tell you the truth,
on this Sunday morning
I really don't care.
For there are many worse things
that can happen in this life
than to listen to a child when he swears.

* *Inspired by the film* The Boy in the Striped Pyjamas

EATING TOGETHER

INTRODUCTION TO HOLY COMMUNION (1)

Voice 1:

Once upon a time, long, long ago,
the Jews were the slaves of the ancient Egyptians.
The Jews were seen as a worthless people
and treated very badly.

Voice 2:

'Let my people go!' said Moses, their leader.
'God says you must let his people go.'

Voice 1:

But the pharaoh refused;
so God sent plagues to torment the Egyptians.
The Nile turned to blood and
the Egyptians had no water.
Swarms of insects ate all the crops
and the Egyptians had nothing to eat.
The place was overrun with frogs – slimy creatures.
They brought infection, disease and disaster.

Voice 2:

'Let my people go!' said Moses, their leader.
'God says you must let his people go.'

Voice 1:

God said to the Jews:

Voice 2:

'I've had just about enough of this.
Get yourselves ready to travel.
But first, take the blood of a lamb,
and smear it over the doors of your houses.
I will send death to Egypt,
and the first-born of each of their families will be killed.
But death will pass over the homes of my people:

those whose houses are marked with blood on the doors.
You are my people: I am your God.
I will release you. I will give you freedom. You will be safe.'

Voice 1:

It happened as God said it would.
Death came and it was terrible,
but the Jews were finally given their freedom and release.

Voice 2:

And ever since then,
people have remembered this event with thanksgiving.
Every year they have celebrated the great Passover Feast.

Voice 1:

It reminded them that God had taken this once nothing people
and made them into a something people.

Voice 2:

It reminded them
that it had been God's own choosing
to risk investing in them
even though there were many safer bets around.

Voice 1:

Centuries later, it was this same Passover Feast
that Jesus and his friends were celebrating one night
in a privately rented room in Jerusalem.

Voice 2:

There was not a holy saint among them.
They were a ragtag and bobtail outfit if ever there was one,
and if truth be told, some were not so nimble in the mental department.

Voice 1:

Others were rough and ready –
no way could they all be described as refined.

Voice 2:

There was a traitor there.
And a hot-headed, act-first-think-later
bull-in-a-china-shop man.
His name was Peter.

Voice 1:

Most of them were fishermen.
Not all of them were able to read and write.

Voice 2:

Jesus knew exactly what these guys were like,
and he knew that clever theological argument
wouldn't carry much weight with them at all.

Voice 1:

How could he convince them?
What could he do to assure them?
How could he make them understand
that, after his death,
he would always be by their side?

Voice 2:

An idea came!
His eyes scanned the room
and settled on the bread and wine which were on the table.
The meal! Of course, the meal!
Why didn't I think of it before?
I'll give it new meaning.
I'll give it a new dimension.
I'll imbue it with a significance and a power
so that anyone who chooses to take part in it
will sense and know I am still with them,
having been crucified but simply refusing ever to die.

Voice 1:

Down through long centuries,
this meal has continued to be celebrated
by his followers and friends.

Voice 2:

All of them imperfect;
many believing they were not good enough;
not one with a total understanding of the power of the meal.

Voice 1:

Seekers, doubters, scoffers, cynics,
yet God calling them to his table
to feast together.

INTRODUCTION TO HOLY COMMUNION (2)

Voice 1:

Those who were at the first meal were very ordinary folk: fishermen, civil servants, income tax collectors and the like. One or two of the older ones may have been retired for all we know.

Voice 2:

There's no question that many of them were apprehensive about the future: they weren't stupid, and could read at least some of the writing on the wall. Others had more than a slight inclination that a major change was about to take place, and suspected that, very shortly, nothing in their lives would ever be the same again.

Voice 1:

So probably some of their laughter that night was nervous laughter: an outward veneer of celebration masked inner apprehension, and fear and concern. For all we know the point may have been reached when their conversations became heated and even acrimonious, for the same thing had happened several times before. Who knows? Perhaps

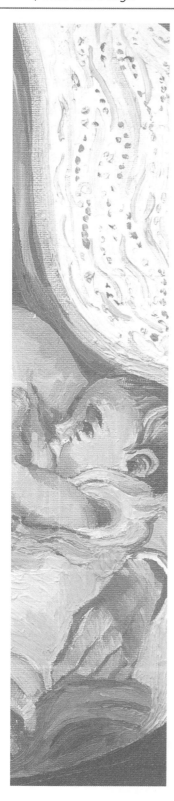

some lacked the grace to be kind to each other, or were the type who nursed resentment, or went off in the huff at the drop of a hat.

Voice 2:

Jesus, perceptive as always, recognised the anxiety, registered the fear, foresaw the potential danger in the changes they would be forced to confront. What could he do about it? What could he say that would hearten them, and provide reassurance, since he knew for sure he would have to leave them within a matter of hours?

Voice 1:

This bread, he thought. *I'll tell them it stands for my body, and that if they keep on sharing the bread, this will prevent them from falling apart. And the wine: I'll say it stands for the new reconciliation between God and the people he loves. And if they accept this, and understand some of what I mean; if they take this truth personally, and are fully on board with it, then whatever big changes happen, at least in themselves they will be safe and secure.*

Voice 2:

So that night, Jesus gave them something he knew would hold them together despite their individual differences. For sharing the bread and wine together undercuts and overrides apartness. It works to unite God's own people as one.

Voice 1:

For this community of faith of ours, there is nothing more important than this sacred, symbolic meal. For the Body of Christ, there is nothing more important than sharing the body and blood of Christ. Here is the most powerful means of holding us together, because we hold out and share with our neighbour nothing less than the generous food of highest heaven.

INTRODUCTION TO HOLY COMMUNION (3)

It is not only the ordained who are able to lead the sacrament of Holy Communion. Large parts of this litany can be led by others as well:

Voice 1:

I remember it only too well:
that night when we sat around the table with him.
Everything was ready;
all the preparations had been carefully made.

Voice 2:

Up until that point, it wasn't all that clear
his methods would make a lasting impression.
Oh, there were the healings of course,
and the so-called miracles, and the blessings he gave
as he roamed all over the place as an itinerant preacher.
They certainly left their mark
on those who benefited from them.
But he wasn't the only one doing this kind of thing –
there were scores of preacher-healers just like him.

Voice 3:

Up until that point, it was anything but clear
that his ministry had been successful.
If universal popularity were to be used as the measure,
then he was a definite failure, for the establishment
(those who controlled and pulled the strings)
hated and detested him.
But then, no wonder.
He said unwise things
when he should have kept quiet.
His criticism of the establishment
was as constant as it was merciless.
He even told them their religion
was rotten to the core.

Voice 1:

I remember it only too well.
That last night, when we sat around the table with him,
I wondered whether this Jesus of Nazareth
would just be another 'nine-day' wonder,
remembered only until the next spectacular attraction arrived on the scene.

Voice 2:

But then he said something very strange,
and while none of us appreciated
the genius of his words at the time,
2000 years of history have shown
that his unconventional ministry
was an unparalleled and unprecedented success.

Voice 3:

And you know,
all he said to us at the meal that night was this:
'Do this to remember me.
Do this to remember me.
Do this to remember me,
and I will be there for you whenever you need me.'

Voice 4:

Many times now, we have heard
about how Jesus shared a meal with his friends:
to show how closely he belonged to them;
to demonstrate how much he longed to be with them.
For he knew what it was to be human,
and wherever his friends were in their living,
he had been there in that same place too.

At the last meal, he broke the bread and poured the wine:
signs of his love;
signs by which they would be able to remember him.

He asked those who were there that night
to keep on meeting together to share;
to continue to eat the bread and drink the wine
so that he could be especially near:
so that he could weep if they were weeping;
and laugh if they were laughing;
so he could comfort and encourage and affirm.

Today we have come to take part in the meal.
And here is something that can help us
in our striving to do the right thing.

Here is something that can make our decision-making
that little bit easier.

Here is something which can give us strength;
and inspire us with intention;
and give us encouragement
to keep us on the right track in all our living.
Here we receive the gifts of heaven:
gifts for the good of us all.

THE DINNER DANCE

This was prepared as an ecumenical service for the Week of Prayer for Christian Unity. Adapt as necessary.

Open sandwiches, appetisers, wine and soft drinks were laid out on the communion table prior to the service.

Comment

The God who surprises very often shocks us by the way he operates and in the demands he makes of his friends. *'The way I think is not how you think. My ways are nothing like your ways at all,'* he says. God surprises us by revealing himself in the most unlikely places; in the most unlikely people. Our God is a God of surprises.

I'd like to take a leaf out of his book tonight and invite you to surprise yourself by dancing in our worship here together! Liturgical dance is very biblical, and there are several places in our scriptures where we can read about people dancing to celebrate their togetherness and their gratitude and thanksgiving. They dance because they believe it gives pleasure to God.

Go to a country like Africa – and the folk there simply can't remain still when they hear music or open their mouths to sing. Feet tap in time, hips move from side to side in rhythm, hands are joined together as people worship their God. I know we're not in Africa, but 'are you dancing, because I'm asking'? Are you up for surprising yourself tonight, and for surprising God too by breaking out of your straightjacket and doing something completely out of character for we Scots, who are thirled to doing everything decently and in good order, and who are usually more comfortable operating at a cerebral rather than emotional level in our worship?

Are you prepared to dance for joy to celebrate the thrilling fact that there are meaningful and positive and healthy and lively relationships of interconnectedness between the people who make up the different congregations in this town? For that truly is something worth celebrating. I'll teach you the steps – they're easy.

The dance: ('Jesu, tawa pano', CH4 773)

Form a circle (or several circles). As each line of the song is sung, 4 steps are taken in time with the music:

Jesu, tawa pano: 2 steps forward, then 2 steps back
Jesu, tawa pano: 2 steps back, then 2 steps forward
Jesu, tawa pano: 2 steps to the right, then 2 steps to the left
Tawa pano, mu zita renyu: 2 steps to the left, then 2 steps to the right

Reading: Matthew 9:9–13

Comment

He upset them. He shocked them big time by sharing food in the houses of low-lifes and riff-raff. And the Pharisees ask: 'What's he doing sitting at the tables of people like that?'

We are dealing with a God of surprises; a God who often:

- surprises us by his words, which make demands that don't suit us; yet we are called to respond

- surprises us by the manner of his presence in people we might not instinctively warm to and naturally gravitate towards, yet we are called to love

- surprises us by continually calling us into communion with each other, and so into closer communion with Jesus. And isn't it great that huge progress has been made, and continues to be made, in this respect; that there is now so much co-operation between congregations and denominations?

But worshipping together can, in a sense, be the very thing that prevents further unity between our communities of faith. Indeed, one of the greatest barriers to further unity often lies in what all believe to be the most central, sacred and treasured element of our worship – the Eucharist, the Mass, the Breaking of the Bread, the Communion, the Lord's Supper. Despite all the clever arguments, there is something wrong – something very badly wrong – when our doctrines and theologies prevent us from sitting at the same table, or kneeling at the same altar; and I can't imagine God smiles approvingly about this at all.

But it isn't only our inability to share the bread and the wine. It's even when we come together like this that the very act of worshipping can conspire to work against us. For we come in, we probably sit beside others of our own congregation; and we go away at the end still strangers to those whose names we don't know. Our forms of worship don't really provide opportunity for personal relationships of connectedness to be established. Another surprise then! A chance to put that right, here and now, by sharing in a symbolic meal together. Help yourself to the food and the wine, and talk to someone you don't know. Just a wee blether: no more than that; no agenda at all. But by the end, make sure at least that you are aware of the other person's name.

Eating together was really important for Jesus. He saw food and drink as having a huge potential to draw people closer. All the time we read about him sitting at tables in people's houses.

We'll share food together now, and maybe God will surprise us as we do this with the folk who surround us today.

Eating and sharing together

Prayer

Sung response: 'Come now, O Prince of Peace' (CH4 275)

Voice 1:

God of surprises, working to unite your people,
yet honouring their uniqueness and differences;
drawing together the single threads, important as they are,
but often weak and vulnerable in their individuality;
weaving them into the attractiveness of the tartan
so they become stronger and more of use in your cause.
Come now, O God of love, make us one body.

Sung response: 'Come now, O Prince of Peace'

Voice 2:

We pray for your church,
often unwilling to listen to what you are saying;
in its sophistication believing it has a monopoly
on your mind and purpose and will;
sometimes struggling in desperation to understand your intention;
wrestling with what it wants to be
as a force for goodness and Godness in the world.
Come now, God of love, and surprise us:
mend our brokenness and set your hurting people free.

Sung response: 'Come now, O Prince of Peace'

Voice 3:

We give you our best song, our most lively dance,
and not least, our deepest thanksgiving
for the sense of togetherness
that exists between the congregations in this town;
for the encouraging willingness there has been
to open minds and lift horizons
and dream the dreams of what yet might be;
for the readiness to examine ourselves and what we are,
and imagine what we could become;
for the realisation that separateness and division
is not part of the Gospel of Jesus Christ,
and the appreciation that great strength is ours for the taking
through the love that comes from heaven
to live beside us here on this earth.

Voice 4:

Keep us lively, keep us keen,
but above all keep our eyes fixed on you,
Prince of Peace, Lord of the Dance,
Hope of Unity and Togetherness and Love.

Sung response: 'Come now, O Prince of Peace'

Song: 'Lord of the dance' (CH4 404)

Dismissal and blessing
(Invite people to hold hands)

Be aware of the hands you hold now:
the hand on your right; the hand on your left;
feel the touch, the texture, the pressure;
different from your hands,
yet the hands of people who are here
because they know the love of the God
who unites his people in his care and compassion.

Then, honour these hands which hold your hands,
for they belong to someone
from whom God means you to receive.
And honour those hands too
since you are to be a giver in return.

And as you go from this place,
take with you the blessing of the Father
to give you security;
the blessing of the Son
who shows you how;
the blessing of the Spirit
who might surprise and irritate you,
for the ways of heaven are not the same as the ways of the earth.

MY GIFT IS ME

This piece is obviously appropriate where children share in the sacrament of Holy Communion.

A child:

Jesus invites me to his table and these are the gifts I bring with me: surprises and excitement and wide-eyed innocence ... and questions: never-ending questions.

You won't have to be worried about getting stuck in your ways or resting on your laurels or getting too comfortable when I'm around. Things may not always go as you expected, but you will never be bored either. Jesus said: 'Let the little children come to me and don't stop them.' He also said the kingdom of heaven belongs to me.

My gift is me, and I bring my heart.

A teenager:

Jesus invites me to his table and these are the gifts I bring with me: restlessness, rebellion and a burning sense of justice ... and questions: never-ending questions.

Where do I fit in this great big puzzle? Where is my place in this body, the church? You probably worry about me, but I'm just trying to find my way. Sometimes I get stuck and feel uncomfortable, but I bring an uncompromising honesty. I expect a lot, and I'm easily bored.

Jesus was restless and rebellious and had a burning sense of justice too. He wrestled with who he was and what his place was, and he definitely expected a lot. He said that the kingdom of God is right here with us, but we have to search for it. He said the kingdom of heaven belongs to me.

My gift is me, and I bring my heart.

An adult:

Jesus invites me to his table and these are the gifts I bring with me: stability, common sense and a roundness which comes from having some of my rough edges smoothed by time.

I come aware I don't know as much as I thought I did. And just when I think I have all the answers, I still have questions: never-ending questions. I wonder about where I'm going, and about the future of the church.

You probably worry about me, because I'm still trying to find my way. Sometimes I get stuck and feel uncomfortable, but I bring an understanding that there are always two sides to every story. I think a lot, and I have learned the art of patience.

Jesus told stories, fed crowds and always had time for the children. He calls us to follow his example, and I'm trying, though I don't always get it right. He said the kingdom of God was all around us, and in the business of my life I have found this is true. The kingdom is right here with us, but we have to search for it. He said the kingdom of heaven belongs to me.

My gift is me, and I bring my heart.

An older person:

Jesus invites me to his table and these are the gifts I bring with me: wisdom and experience and a long-earned sense of self.

I may be a bit past my sell-by date, but it helps me to be honest and open: I don't have so much to prove. Don't assume that just because I'm old I'm stuck in my ways or resting on my laurels, or getting too comfortable. I'm not settling down for a long winter's nap, and I don't want to be bored either.

God has never been ageist. Since the beginning of time he has had a tendency to call older folk to do new things. Abraham and Sarah were collecting their pensions when they had Isaac. Simeon and Anna were waiting to see God in heaven when they were surprised by Jesus in the temple.

Life is full of ups and downs, but there is one thing I'm certain about: you're never too old for questions. Questions are never ending. 'The old ones will dream dreams.' That's what God said. The kingdom of heaven belongs to me.

My gift is me, and I bring my heart.

Sally Foster-Fulton

CONVERSATIONS

TELL US HOW AND WHY AND WHEN

Song: 'Be still and know that I am God' (CH4 754)

Human words, however clever, can never be enough
to tell of your wonder, explain your mystery,
celebrate your power.
For you are the God who made this world and all its people:
who formed us and knitted us together in our mother's womb.

We can sing your praises;
we can wax lyrical about your greatness;
we can proclaim as loud as we like that you are God of all.
And yet, we know that the best depth of our worship
is often found in the speechless quietness of our imagining;
the most profound communion with you
discovered in the voiceless silence.

So then, we will be still.
We will be still and listen to your voice.
We will be still so we can know that you are our God.

Song: 'Be still and know that I am God'

Since the beginning, you have always remained
with and beside your people:
healing their hurts,
holding their hands,
drying their tears.

When they have acknowledged their brokenness
and the fragility of their humanity,
you have smiled, and warmly welcomed.

When they have told you about their regrets,
and shared their fears and disappointments,
you have cuddled and affirmed and reassured.

And even in the worst times,
when apprehension about the future
disrupts the contentment and peace of the present,

you have said: 'Be still. Know I am your God.
I love you, and I love you more than you can ever know.'

Song: 'Be still and know that I am God'

And so in the silence of this place now,
speak, and we will listen.
Let us hear your gentle, kindly voice.
Meet our needs,
answer our questions,
respond to our worries and concerns.

Great God,
talk to each one here intimately, secretly, personally,
and tell us how,
and tell us why,
and tell us when.

Time of silence

The voice of God has spoken.
We are his, and he is ours.
Thanks be to God.
Amen

WITH THE HAND OF AN ARTIST

Voice 1:

You have made us:
not as two-dimensional simple souls,
not as cloned and cardboard cut-outs,
flat and shallow and without any depth.
Instead, with the hand of an artist you have shaped us,
invested your people with creativity and sensitivity,
and you have given us passion and feeling as well.
Such gifts you mean us to use
to tell your story; to demonstrate your meaning;
to share your love with those who walk beside and around us.

Song: 'Glory and gratitude and praise' (*Come All You People*)

Voice 2:

In the rhythm of a beating heart we sense you.
When two lovers meet, and no words are needed, there you are.
When death does its worst, or a look says it all;
when the cries of the poor sing a jarring melody in our ears;
and when discordant cries for justice
disturb and disrupt our pleasant dreaming,
you are here, you are there, you are now.

Song: 'Glory and gratitude and praise'

Voice 1:

In the harmony that is all of creation we meet you:
as the snowflake's symmetry melts into water;
as the buds push through the warming springtime earth;
when birth and death are held in sacred tension;
when we are moved to compassion by the sight and sound of pain;
you are here, you are there, you are now.

Song: 'Glory and gratitude and praise'

Voice 2:

In the counterpoint of this world's being we feel you:
when yes and no, and good and bad compete;
when selflessness and greed dance together as partners;
when threatening fists do irreparable damage to eyes which smile in welcome.
When forgiveness is offered so that Godness breathes and lives again,
you are here, you are there, you are now.

Song: 'Glory and gratitude and praise'

Voice 1:

In this great symphony that is our living together –
in the syncopation that adds interest and colour to all our days;

through the tempo at which we move
or stand rooted in stillness –
let your earth discover its harmony and satisfying resolution
which is no less than your love.

Song: 'Glory and gratitude and praise'

THE THRONE ROOM OF HEAVEN

The place is the New Jerusalem: the heavenly city.
The scene is the throne room of the holy, sacred temple;
that awesome place where the God of all the universe resides.

Angels and archangels surround the throne;
cherubim and seraphim throng the air;
the great multitude of saints and sinners
of all the ages make up the choir.
They sing their eternal song of praise:

Holy, holy, holy Lord,
God of power and might.
Heaven and earth are full of your glory.
Hosanna in the highest!

The sound makes the very ground beneath your feet tremble.
The solid walls shake to their deep foundations.
The temple is filled with smoke:
altar fires are burning around the throne
in tribute to his unsurpassed majesty.
The incense which reaches everywhere
is a symbol of his ubiquitous presence and power.

The song begins again, and you join with them
in worship of the Great Lord of All:

Blessing and honour and glory and power
be unto him who sits upon the throne.
And thanks never ceasing to the One who is infinite Love.

Then there is silence: a sacred silence,
for the Lord has left his throne.
The great crowd in front of you parts to make way for him.
The Lord has left his throne.

He makes his way towards you.
You know he means to welcome you gladly.
You sense the power of the purity of his love and loveliness.
You feel the warmth of his acceptance
which radiates from his presence beside you now.

And even though you are surrounded by this great multitude,
this moment is yours; this moment is his;
for none can hear, and none can see,
and none will ever know
this sacred conversation you are to have with your Lord and God.

Christ Jesus stands before you now,
and love is in his mind.

What does he say?
What does he say?
What does he say to you?

A time of quiet

For this sacred time of holy communion with you,
I worship and adore you,
my gracious and loving, living God.
Amen

HOLY, HOLY, HOLY

Song: 'Holy, holy, holy' (CH4 769)

Different and unique;
your ways not like our ways;
perfect love; absolute goodness;
undiluted beauty and unadulterated truth;
divinity in all its glory and all its power.

High above the earth
yet present in every person.
Wandering where you will,
yet setting up home, and taking up residence
in the hearts of those who know you.
Dying in your humanity;
living in your divinity:
the God we worship;
the God who is holy;
the God who is love.

Song: 'Holy, holy, holy'

Infant voices sing your song in the first cry of their birth.
Those on deathbeds seek and sense you
as they draw their last breath.
And in between, millions call on your name
in times of gladness,
in times of happiness,
in times of pain.
God of them all,
and God of us too,
you are heaven's presence of love here on this earth.

Song: 'Holy, holy, holy'

And now is the time,
and here is the place
when we can come closer to you.
We will recall our regrets;

we will share with you our fears;
we will tell you about our dreams.
Listen kindly, great love, listen kindly.
And be gentle in your response,
and lavish your mercy on us.
Be generous with your smiles of acceptance
and free with your welcoming words.

Time of quiet

You have forgiven and you have encouraged;
you have affirmed and you have rebuked;
you have cautioned and you have kindled enthusiasm.
Then in response to all your mercy and all your goodness,
we are glad to say the words: You are holy, Lord.

Song: 'Holy, holy, holy'

SUMMON OUT WHAT I CAN BE

Song: 'Take, oh, take me as I am' (CH4 795)

Voice 1:

Jesus, God incarnate, living love,
healing and mending brokenness;
giving blind folk sight; insight;
showing those paralysed by themselves
how to leap and dance again;
miracle-worker who releases from self-imposed captivity
prisoners who have forgotten how and what it is to live.
Look kindly on your people gathered here;
identify what is lacking in us;
and work your work so we might become
all that heaven intends.

Song: 'Take, oh, take me as I am'

Voice 2:

Jesus, God incarnate, living love;
restorer and reshaper;
life creator and new-life maker;
look kindly on your people gathered here,
and see all the potential that remains dormant and unused
for love lies latent within is.
Summon out the best in us:
the way we might care for each other more gently;
the way we might be more generous with our time;
the way we might support your precious people
in all their difficulties.
Release the energy from within us
so we can help others to live life to the full.

Song: 'Take, oh, take me as I am'

Voice 3:

Jesus, God incarnate, living love;
set your seal upon our hearts,
so that we are more willing
to embrace the pain and needs of a suffering world,
for many are disabled
by those whose intention is to direct and control.
Many are too weak to stand up for themselves against authority.
Many have no other option but to do as they are told.
And many, far, far too many,
are forced into only existing,
and no more than that.

Summon out the good in us,
to work new miracles for you,
by taking your light, your hope, your freedom,
your peace and your security
to those who don't know it,
and who need heaven's power to make their being
more content and complete.

Song: 'Take, oh, take me as I am'

NEITHER RACE NOR GENDER

Neither race nor gender,
neither wisdom nor age,
neither strength of faith nor lack of certainty
make the slightest bit of difference to you.

You welcome one, you welcome all.
You welcome friends, you welcome strangers.
One and all you care for and love
with the deepest passion of your heart and your soul.

When there are tears, you help to dry them.
When there is laughter, you always join in.
When there are hopes, you inspire and encourage them.
And when there is grace and compassion in sharing,
your heart skips a beat like an infatuated lover.

Great God, as individuals
who belong to this community of faith,
we have gathered together to worship you.
For we sense your goodness;
we have experience of your unending faithfulness;
we have knowledge of your power that amends our living.
Once again we lift our voices to praise you
for all you have done, and continue to do,
for your precious, beloved people.

Creation too, in all its delicate beauty,
sings your glorious song.
Birds build bedrooms to nurture their babies:
they reflect your God-like protection.
All creatures great and small
are echoes of your image.
And all people,
rich and poor and young and old,
are the children of highest heaven.

In gratitude, in thanksgiving, in appreciation,
in expectation that you will give us even more,
for that is your way,

then let this house, and every other house,
proclaim from floor to rafter:
All are welcome!

But come closer to us now,
and take from our souls
the strain and the stress we may have brought here this day.
Remove our guilt, lessen our regret,
and help us to deal sensibly with our brokenness.
Fill us with hope and dreams of the future.
God will you meet us, and make us new again?

Time of silence

The one who longs to make us whole
has saved us from ourselves.
The one who soothes our troubled souls
gives life and peace and blessing.
Thanks be to God.

JESUS, I'M AFRAID

Voice 1:

Jesus, I'm afraid.
Nothing is as it once was;
everything around me is different.
So many of the familiar things I have known
are under threat or have already disappeared.
The world is just not the same as it used to be.

Song: 'Don't be afraid' (*Come All You People*, or CH4 191, chorus only)

Voice 2:

Jesus, I'm afraid.
The changes are unsettling and upsetting,
and often it feels as if things are spiralling out of control.
The comfortable landmarks and signposts are being removed.
It's like being in a ship without a sail on a dangerous sea.

Song: 'Don't be afraid'

Voice 3:

Jesus, I'm afraid too.
I know there's something sinister growing inside me.
I can tell by the look on people's faces my chances are slim.
Please, let your resurrection story be true
and let it be real for me.
Please don't let the long sleep of death be all that there is.

Song: 'Don't be afraid'

Voice 4:

Jesus, I'm afraid.
The dark clouds of war are gathering.
They just won't listen when we plead: 'Look for another way.'
They will warp the beauty and truth of heaven's precious creation.
The heartbreak and pain of your wounded people
will be hellish and fierce.

Song: 'Don't be afraid'

Voice 5:

Jesus, I'm afraid.
The past which I long for is now irrecoverable.
The future which I imagine is threatening and insecure.
My fear for the present is real: I live and breathe it.
In the silence, will you give me heaven's reassurance,
and in our communion, in your mercy,
give me heaven's own peace?

Time of silence

Song: 'Don't be afraid'

Voice 6:

God, take our fear away.
Let us know the strength of your love.
Give us the faith to trust you.
And let each one of us here know you and sense you;
and convince us that you are always close and near.

PRACTICAL THEOLOGY

Before the service, prepare five stations around the church. Place short pieces of knotted string at one, some stones at the second, small votive candles (or tea-lights) at the third, snappable twigs at the fourth and some sweets at the fifth station (enough for the whole congregation). Place a lighted candle at each station, and an empty cross on the communion table.

Comment 1

Unless our theology is practical theology, it is of no use to neither man nor beast. Unless all the fine theories of doctrine and philosophies of religion are grounded, earthed and firmly rooted in what people actually experience in their living, then all such talk is nothing more than rarefied, academic blether which takes place in a vacuum. For example:

- It's one thing to claim we love a person, but that love has to be demonstrated in practical ways before it can be seen to be true.

- It is easy to claim to be generous, but the only real proof of this is if we actually write a cheque, or dip into our pockets and share. In that way the theory doesn't simply remain a theory.

That was the very point Jesus was making when, one day, he gave them a verbal beating up. They said all the right things, but neglected to practise what they preached.

Reading: Matthew 23: 1–3, 13–15, 25–26 (GNB)

Then Jesus spoke to the crowds and to his disciples. 'The teachers of the Law and the Pharisees are the authorised interpreters of Moses' Law. So you must obey and follow everything they tell you to do; do not, however, imitate their actions, because they don't practise what they preach ...

'How terrible for you, teachers of the Law and Pharisees! You hypocrites! You lock the door to the Kingdom of heaven in people's faces, but you yourselves don't go in, nor do you allow in those who are trying to enter! How terrible for you, teachers of the Law and Pharisees! You hypocrites! You sail the seas and cross whole countries to win one convert; and when you succeed, you make him twice as deserving of going to hell as you yourselves are! ...

'How terrible for you, teachers of the Law and Pharisees! You hypocrites! You clean the outside of your cup and plate, while the inside is full of what you have gotten by violence and selfishness. Blind Pharisee! Clean what is inside the cup first, and then the outside will be clean too!' ...

Comment 2

Various items have been placed at five 'work' stations around the church. In a few minutes, I will invite you to visit these places.

At the first station, there's a basket with pieces of string in it, each with a knot. The knot represents a knot that might reside somewhere inside you, because there is someone, or even a group of people, you have just not been able to forgive. It could be that you hold a grudge against them, or are bitter or resentful because of something they've said or done in the past. Maybe they insulted you. Maybe they talked about you behind your back. Maybe they said something that really wounded, and you were perfectly right to be annoyed at the time. If that's you, then take a piece of string. Take it home with you, but don't untie the knot until you know you have reached the point of real forgiveness, and are sure in your own thinking that you have set that person, or persons, completely free.

Forgiveness is for our own benefit, and for our own wholesomeness we have to know how to forgive, otherwise we end up being bitter and twisted inside. Here's what Jesus said about this important matter:

Reading: Matthew 18:21–22 (GNB)

Then Peter came to Jesus and asked, 'Lord, if my brother keeps on sinning against me, how many times do I have to forgive him? Seven times?' 'No, not seven times,' answered Jesus, 'but seventy times seven.' ...

Comment 3

The guilt people carry is like nobody's business: it can screw folk up big time, and often it debilitates and diminishes to the extent that it prevents individuals from blossoming into the kind of people God means them to be. There are more than a few who are only too aware of something they ought to have done but didn't, or something they ought not to have done but did. Many continue to carry guilt for this, and it is like a millstone around their neck.

At the second station, stones stand for this weight of guilt that people carry. Take a stone if you are one of those people. Take it home with you, and when you have reached the point when you realise God has forgiven you completely, absolutely, then throw the stone away. And let that be an indicator that you know you are restored, and set free from yourself once again.

Song: 'We will lay our burden down' (*Love from Below*)

Reading: John 21:15–17 (GNB)

After they had eaten, Jesus said to Simon Peter, 'Simon son of John, do you love me more than these others do?' 'Yes, Lord,' he answered, 'you know that I love you.' Jesus said to him, 'Take care of my lambs.'

A second time Jesus said to him, 'Simon son of John, do you love me?' 'Yes, Lord,' he answered, 'you know that I love you.' Jesus said to him, 'Take care of my sheep.'

A third time Jesus said, 'Simon son of John, do you love me?' Peter became sad because Jesus asked him the third time, Do you love me? and so he said to him, 'Lord, you know everything; you know that I love you!' Jesus said to him, 'Take care of my sheep.'

Comment 4

At the third station, there are candles, and they also are for taking away: to be lit as a reminder of those words of Jesus: 'Take care of my lambs ... Take care of my sheep.' It is our calling and intended destiny as followers of the Way to have concern for all sorts of people in this world. Maybe this is one of the areas where putting theory into practice is tested the hardest. While we agree to the principle of active caring very readily, some-

times we can forget it or ignore it or let it lapse.

If you think the caring candle is for you, take it away, and use it as inspiration to encourage you to consider where and in what very specific way you might turn the theory into practice for yourself. Is it a cheque to Christian Aid? Is it something that needs to be done for one of your neighbours? Is there someone who is struggling and could do with help? Or is there another avenue you might pursue to show that you care?

Song: 'Brother, sister let me serve you' (CH4 694)

Reading: Matthew 5:43–48 (GNB)

'You have heard that it was said, Love your friends, hate your enemies. But now I tell you: love your enemies and pray for those who persecute you, so that you may become the children of your Father in heaven. For he makes his sun to shine on bad and good people alike, and gives rain to those who do good and to those who do evil. Why should God reward you if you love only the people who love you? Even the tax collectors do that! And if you speak only to your friends, have you done anything out of the ordinary? Even the pagans do that! You must be perfect just as your Father in heaven is perfect.'

Comment 5

'You must be perfect,' says Jesus. No, he didn't! What he said was: 'You must be *teleios*.' *Teleios* is a Greek word that means you must fulfil all the potential you are meant to fulfil. 'You must be everything you are supposed to be.' But fulfilling our potential is not the same as being perfect. If we were perfect, our true name would be 'God'.

There is a basket with twigs at the fourth station. They are dry and will snap very easily if you bend them. Is there an aspect of your character you need to work on? What is it about you that you should expend some energy on and try to sort out? Is it meanness? Is it a lack of tolerance or impatience? Is it selfishness? Or is it something else that only you know, and God knows?

Take the twig home, and when you are ready to start working on that particular part of your character, snap the twig, as a sign that you are about to start working on it seriously.

Song: 'Spirit of the living God, fall afresh on me' (CH4 619)

Comment 6

At the fifth station, there's a basket of sweets. Everybody has to take one. Whatever we are, whatever we've done, whatever we could be, we have to know our God loves us with all of his heart. Sometimes it can be hard for us to love ourselves. And yet, right at the beginning of the story of God, there is a repeated refrain which proclaims: 'God made the world and said "It is good".'

God loves the world he made. More than anything, God loves the people he made. As you eat the sweet, whenever you eat the sweet, either now or later, be reminded of that, and know that, as far as God is concerned, you are more precious than the finest gold.

Reading: John 15:9–10 (GNB)

'I love you just as the Father loves me; remain in my love. If you obey my commands, you will remain in my love, just as I have obeyed my Father's commands and remain in his love.'

Visiting the stations/time of personal reflection

People are invited to visit the various stations. After a time of personal reflection, music signals them to gather together at the communion table.

Comment 7

There's one last object I want us to consider: the empty cross. The cross has become probably the most important Christian symbol, and crosses similar to this one on our communion table can be seen in churches the world over. The theory is that the cross on which Jesus died became empty and remained empty. But how do we know that is true? How do we know Jesus resurrected? How do we know Jesus is still alive?

For a start, you and I are here tonight, and that simple fact is enough: no more needs to be said: The living Spirit of God, alive in your heart and in mine, affecting who we are and what we do: there is resurrection. That is what is meant by the word resurrection, and no more proof is needed.

But how do we go about convincing folk this is not simply a theory? The only way to do it is to put the theory into practice: to display the powerful truth of the resurrection in the way we lead our lives. And if it takes a piece of string, or a stone, or a candle, or a bit of twig, or even a sweetie to help us to do that, then our time here tonight has not been wasted.

Song: 'Christ is alive!' (CH4 416)

SECRETS

For this group reflection, collect a piece of driftwood from the shore, or a decaying piece of wood from a forest. Depending on its attributes, prepare your own comments and observations. Then comment on the wood, drawing on the points below, as appropriate.

Shape

- Complete lack of consistency in shape
- Totally random in contour
- Not a straight line to be seen
- No two curves are the same
- Covered in recesses and prominences
- No symmetry here at all

Texture

- Great variety in texture
- Some parts smooth and silky; others rough and gnarled

Colour

- Many different shades
- Interesting natural lack of consistency

Pattern

- Comprises a collection of mini-patterns
- In some places parallel lines
- In other places lines running at different angles
- Not much straightness to be seen

Centre of gravity

- Asymmetrical so possesses a number of centres of gravity
- Happily sits on different angles and planes

Unknowns

- What kind of wood is it?
- How old is it?
- How have indentations been formed?
- Why are some parts rough and other parts smooth?
- Which part of the tree did it form?
- How high above the ground did it grow?

What does it say to us?

- Stare at it and it might look pleasing
- Or else you might feel it looks a bit sinister
- Is there a face to be seen – a rabbit, a troll, a pig?

So much could be said about this unique piece of wood: so much could be said about each of us as individual human beings, every last one of us totally unique.

We could consider:

- our own shape and contour (or we may prefer not to!)
- the texture of our personality: the rough and smooth bits
- the way we are inconsistent or asymmetrical in our behaviour and actions
- the puzzling aspects of our character ('Why did I do that?') since sometimes we don't understand ourselves.

So there are lots of parallels which could be drawn. But I want to ask you to focus on only one particular aspect of your own personality now. This piece of wood is covered in many little holes and recesses. Some are superficial and shallow; others are fairly deep. Here, here and here there are really deep indentations, and there's room for something to be well hidden in them.

Which part of you are you always anxious to keep hidden from others?
What aspect of your character are you most dissatisfied with or ashamed of?
What about yourself would you most like to change?
If you were having a conversation with God, what might you say about this to him?
And what do you think he might say about it to you?

Time of reflection

Psalm 139 reminds us that even though we may wish to keep part of ourselves hidden, there is no part of our thinking or nature which God does not have access to or is not aware of. It is a good theology that teaches us there is no place that God cannot be. If this is the case, then divinity's sphere of operation and presence and knowledge must encompass and include every last one of our most personal and private deepest secrets.

Song: 'You are before me, God' (Psalm 139) (CH4 96)

BLESS THE LORD, MY SOUL

This needs to be taken at a very slow pace, with good long pauses.

Voice 1:

Think back to when you woke up this morning.
Picture yourself lying in the security of your own cosy bed.
Think of the rooms in your house,
and all the comforts that make life easy.
Think of the people you live with,
or if you are alone,
the friends or family who care for you.
Think of these things, and thank God for them all.

(Pause)

Voice 2:

Think back to when you washed this morning.
Think of the water from the tap, conveniently flowing;
the smell of the shampoo and soap which cleaned you;
the taste of the toothpaste in your mouth – refreshing.
Think of the easiness of your living
when so many are forced to struggle.
Think of these things, and thank God for them all.

(Pause)

Voice 3:

Think back to when you dressed this morning:
the suits in the wardrobe;
the jerseys in the drawer;
all the garments you were able to choose from.
Think of their touch and texture;
their colour and variety;
their familiarity and their newness too,
when so many own only the rags they stand up in.
Think of these things, and thank God for them all.

(Pause)

Voice 1:

Generous and giving God,
so much we have,
so little we notice,
so often we take it all for granted.
The beauty of this earth: we ignore it.
The beating of our heart: we don't think about it.
The care that surrounds us,
the love that is given to us,
the compassion and forgiveness that is ours to share.

Voice 2:

Bless the Lord, O my soul.
All that is in me be stirred up
to magnify and bless his holy name.

Voice 3:

O my soul, bless the Lord,
and do not forget all the gracious benefits
he has bestowed on you.

Voices 1, 2, 3:

Bless the Lord, O my soul.

IN THE MYSTERIES OF LIFE WE MEET YOU

In the mysteries of life we meet you:
in the intensities of the silences;
in the sudden realisation of the power of love;
in the beauty we stumble upon,
which makes us stop and catch our breath, and wonder.
And in the relationships that are ours,
where you are present when tenderness is shared,
which helps us to sense something
of the meaning of being.

So there you are, and here we are,
catching glimpses of you, and being startled
in the glory of precious, sacred moments.

Faithful God of love,
saving God who renews us,
we confess our regrets;
we share with you our most optimistic dreaming;
and we bring to you all our hurts and all our bruising.
And this we do confidently, because you understand:
you understand us better than we understand ourselves.

Time of quiet

For running away from your love, you forgive us.
For preferring the safe and familiar, you forgive us.
For refusing to believe in your power, you forgive us.
For not being prepared to transform ourselves
and reach the potential for which we were made, you forgive us.

And because from this moment we are new people,
born again, and given yet another chance to live,
so with heaven, and earth, and all creation
we praise and bless your holy name.

TRULY, MADLY, DEEPLY

Comment

If you've never fallen in love with someone – and I'm talking truly, madly, deeply, head-over-heels in love – then you might find what I am about to say less easy to understand. But the fact that you've not had that experience doesn't make you any less of a person, of course. Nor does it mean that somehow you've missed out, or that your living has been in some way incomplete, for countless numbers of people on this earth find a sense of real personal fulfilment in any number of ways which have nothing to do with being part of a one-to-one relationship. So if you've never been there, bear with me as I try to put into words what others might have felt when they found themselves falling deeply, madly in love:

- Do you remember those days, the rest of you? Maybe it was a long time ago, or maybe not. But do you still remember how your heart turned over, and literally missed a beat?

- Do you remember what it was like when you just couldn't help yourself, and in a sense lost control of your emotions and feelings?

- Do you remember when your mind became completely one-track, and everything else in your life moved into second place, because of this insistent, overwhelming compulsion to be close to the only one you wanted to be with – the one you desperately needed to be part of your life for evermore?

Do you remember that time, those of you who have been there? And can you grasp at least something of what it is like, those of you who haven't?

It's scary. The power of love takes over completely, and people will go to almost any length, and move heaven and earth as a consequence. They'll give up their job; they'll move to another country; they'll risk breaking well-established ties of relationship with family and lifelong friends. And some have even been prepared to die for the sake of this thing called love. And if it so happens the love is only one-sided, and not returned, then there can be disaster. For the future can seem pointless and without any purpose, and the present holds no joy or pleasure.

What a tremendously powerful force it is. In fact, there is nothing we humans know of that is any more powerful or any more life-amending. So I'm right up there with St Paul when he says: 'Yes, there's faith and hope as well. But without question, the greatest is love.'

Now in case you think I'm getting all nauseatingly Mills & Boon romantic, or *People's Friend* smushy and sentimental, let me tell you where all of this is heading.

The Old Testament book that now goes by the title Song of Songs used to be known as Song of Solomon, until somebody discovered the wise King Solomon couldn't possibly have written it, since the language it uses comes from a much later period. So Song of Songs is usually how it's referred to now.

But when they were first trying to decide which ancient writings should be included in the Bible, and which should be left out, Song of Songs only just made it by the skin of its teeth. And that was because nowhere does it make any mention of God. Nor is there any reference to things like faith or belief or heaven. Instead, Song of Songs is a series of beautiful love poems which take the form of very intimate and personal conversations between a man and a woman; a man and a woman who have fallen very deeply in love. The woman says this to him:

Your lips cover me with kisses;
your love is better than wine.
There is a fragrance about you;
the sound of your name recalls it.
No woman could help loving you.
Take me with you, and we'll run away.
Be my king, and take me to your room.
We will be happy together,
drink deep, and lose ourselves in love.

Well, there's no mistaking her feelings there and no question about the depth of her passion, or indeed the heat of her desire for him. He is the first and last thing on her mind. Fortunately for her, he feels the same way. It's clear he is equally besotted because this is what he says in response:

How beautiful you are, my love!
How your eyes shine with love behind your veil.
Your hair dances like a flock of goats
bounding down the hills of Gilead.
Your teeth are as white as sheep
that have just been shorn and washed.
Not one of them is missing;
they are all perfectly matched.
Your lips are like a scarlet ribbon;
how lovely they are when you speak.

Your cheeks glow behind your veil.
Your neck is like the tower of David: round and smooth,
with a necklace like a thousand shields hung round it.
Your breasts are like gazelles:
twin deer feeding among the lilies.
I will stay on the hill of myrrh, the hill of incense,
until the morning breezes blow,
and the darkness disappears.
How beautiful you are, my love!
How perfect you are!

Wow! He's certainly smitten with this love thing, though I wonder whether or not she was pleased when he compared her hair to a flock of dancing goats. At least it's good to know she's got all her own sheep-white teeth and doesn't need to rely on dentures!

Did you notice: no mention at all of God in these words. Not a single whisper about his mighty acts, his mercy, his loving-kindness. Little wonder therefore that some didn't want to include this book in the Bible. Unless, we're meant to understand this man and woman's conversation in a different way; unless beneath the surface of what is clearly personal, semi-erotic love poetry we are meant to understand that the conversation actually refers to the relationship – not between a man and a woman – but between God and his people; the people he is truly, madly, deeply, head-over-heels in love with, to the extent that he is actually willing to give up his very own life for them. A song that makes this very point:

Song: 'My song is love unknown' (CH4 399)

Meditation

Song of Songs is understood to be allegorical writing: saying or talking about one thing, while all the time referring to and meaning something completely different. So this book of ancient love poetry has nothing to do with this particular man and woman. They are only archetypes, if you like, and in reality, they probably never even existed. Instead, this writing is about God, and about you and me, and it's saying that you and I are the very heart's desire of the God of heaven.

Now interestingly enough, Song of Songs is very careful *not* to say which of the couple – the man or the woman – is meant to represent God. And that's because we can quite legitimately think of divinity in either way: male or female. Indeed, we can legitimately think of God as being beyond any gender: a power, a force who makes things happen. But for the moment, since physical human gender is all we have to go on, maybe it is easier if we give God arms and legs.

Have you ever thought about God in the way Song of Songs is suggesting?

- God truly, madly, deeply interested in you as a person

- You his/her first thought in the morning and last thought at night

- God incredibly desperate to be beside you

- God longing for your presence

- God aching for the closeness of your company

- God wanting you with all the passion, all the intensity, all the urgency of an utterly besotted and single-minded lover

I invite you to do some imagining now. You might want to close your eyes if it helps. Imagine you are in your own house, sitting in your favourite chair in your living room, the place where you always sit. The house is quiet: there's nobody else in, only you. The telly is switched off, and you're just relaxing; enjoying the peace after a long and busy day.

You hear the outside door opening, and it closes again, and you know someone has come in: someone you have been expecting; someone you have very deep feelings for; someone who means absolutely everything in the world to you. It's not a husband or a wife or a partner. It's not a son, or a daughter or even a very good friend.

The living room door opens and your heart misses a beat. You can feel the excitement welling up inside you. For the one who has come to visit, the one who smiles, the one who sits down beside you, is none other than God, the one who loves you from beginning to end. And these are the words God speaks: words you have been longing to hear:

How wonderful you are, my love, my dearest.
How your eyes shine with love.
Like an apple tree among the trees of the forest,
so are you, compared with others, to me.
Come then, my love, my darling, come with me.
You are mine, and I am yours.
Let me see your face.
Let me hear your enchanting voice,
for you have stolen my heart.
Your love delights me;

your love is better than the finest of wine;
you are one in ten thousand.
Your eyes are as beautiful
as the doves by a flowing brook.
How complete the delights of the love we share.
Everything about you enchants me,
and you are mine, and I am yours for ever and ever.

These are the words of God to you.

These are the personal, intimate words of the one who loves you. But what will you say in return? What will you say in return?

Time of quiet

Spoken psalm *(said together)*:

AS THE THIRSTY DEER PANTS FOR WATER,
SO MY SOUL LONGS FOR YOU.
YOU ALONE ARE MY HEART'S DESIRE,
AND I LONG TO WORSHIP YOU.
I WANT YOU MORE THAN GOLD OR SILVER.
ONLY YOU CAN SATISFY.
YOU ALONE ARE MY REAL JOY-GIVER:
THE APPLE OF MY EYE.
YOU'RE MY FRIEND, MY BROTHER, MY SISTER,
EVEN THOUGH YOU ARE A KING.
I LOVE YOU MORE THAN ANY OTHER;
SO MUCH MORE THAN ANYTHING.
YOU ALONE ARE MY STRENGTH, MY SHIELD;
TO YOU ALONE MAY MY SPIRIT YIELD.
YOU ALONE ARE MY HEART'S DESIRE,
AND I LONG TO WORSHIP YOU.

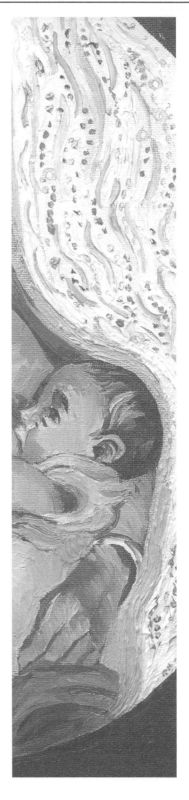

HERE IN THIS SACRED PLACE

Here in this sacred place
many hopes have been heard,
many hearts have been healed,
many regrets have been removed,
many restless minds have found their peace.
Here in this holy place
is where you come close,
and make yourself known
to your people whom you treasure and love.

Song: 'Holy, holy, holy'(CH4 769) (*may be sung by a solo voice*)

Yet this is not the only place,
nor is this the only time
where and when you are present on the earth.
For you are an everywhere God:
beyond space; outside time; outwith dimension;
beyond the boundaries of human understanding;
roving unfettered and free;
your great Spirit amending and reforming,
your will birthing decency and justice and compassionate concern.

Song: 'Holy, holy, holy'

God of heaven, God of earth;
God of each, God of some, God of all;
Great Love, divine Love, live in me.
Let the quietness here be a sacred moment
when we sense and know you.

Take away our fear and replace it with your security.
Take away our regret and replace it with your forgiveness.
Take away our guilt and replace it with your acceptance.
Take away our sadness and replace it with your peace.

Time of quiet

Here in this place you have found us.
Thanks be to you, different and holy one,
God of all this world.

Song: 'Holy, holy, holy'

HOLY GROUND

Invite people to take off their shoes. The pace of this meditation needs to be taken slowly so that the imagery may be absorbed. The response may be sung by a single voice.

Song: 'Be still and know that I am God' (*There Is One Among Us*)

In the silence of this holy place
we will be quiet and we will be still.

For the Great One who made the stars and the sea is here:
he who birthed this world and its people into being.
And so in reverence and gratitude and awe,
we have taken off our shoes as a sign of our respect
for our Maker, and Reshaper, our heavenly Friend.

Song: 'Be still and know that I am God'

There is none beside you.
There is no other like you.
There can be no other to match you.
For you are the one who has come to this earth,
but also has his home in sacred heaven.

And there you sit on your sapphire throne,
surrounded by the great company of angels and archangels,
and all the saints who have gone before us on this earth.

We hear their triumphant hymn of praise
to the one who, in mystery, surpasses all understanding,
and who reigns in majesty, and glory, and eternal power.

And we, confined to this earth at this time,
picture the scene, and join in their song:

Holy, holy, holy Lord,
God of power and might.
Heaven and earth are full of your glory.
Hosanna in the highest!

A time of silence

You are the one who calls us your friends.

Song: 'Be still and know that I am God'

Christ Jesus stands beside us in this place,
and peace is on his mind.
We think of his face,
the colour of his eyes,
the length of his hair,
the shape of the smile on his lips,
his arms outstretched in welcome.

This is your best friend.
He understands you and knows your mind.
He is the one with whom you can share
your deepest secret,
your secret fear,
your most fearful worry.
Christ Jesus stands beside us in this sacred place.
Speak, and he will listen.
Listen, and he will heal.

A time of silence

I am the one whose love never fails.

Song: 'Be still and know that I am God'

Now look out beyond this place
to the world in which you live.
Look out, and see your God is there before you.

In the person you know you should treat more kindly,
see what God is doing in kindness.
In the person who needs your forgiveness,
see how readily God has already forgiven.
In the despised, the rejected, the downtrodden,
see how God affirms, accepts, and lifts them up again.
In the poor, in the have-nots, in the helpless,
see how God gives, and gives again, without reserve.

He calls you to do the same.
He calls you to hold their hands.
He calls you to take off your shoes,
for where they stand is also sacred ground.

A time of silence

He is the one who calls us his friends.
He is the one whose love never fails.
He is our best hope;
our highest purpose;
he lives within us all.

SPIRIT OF TRUTH AND LOVE

Spirit of truth and love,
like an explosion of multi-coloured lights
you break into our thinking and catch us off guard,
and surprise us with the realisation of your meaning.
Incarnate Son of God, weakling child,
quietly and gently you creep in beside us,
and sometimes we catch our breath,
for you take us completely unawares.

Dancing Spirit of energy,
mercurial and dynamic force,
impossible to tie down or make captive,
free as the wind, strong as the sea,
roaming wherever you please.

Great Love, in all of it you are on our side.
Always you want the best for us.
Always your greatest wish:
that our living should be wholesome and complete.

Confidently then, we invite you to come close.
For your love is broader than the measure of any human mind.
Confidently we can confide in you our secrets
for you are our confidant, our easy listener,
our unshockable friend.

So then, come now, and find out all there is to know about me.
Read my thoughts, and probe the depths of my thinking and feeling.

In the quietness now, let us sense you.
In the quietness speak the words we need to hear.

Time of quiet

You made every part of me.
In secret you put me together in my mother's womb.
For who, and all that I am, I praise you:
the one who lives, and lives in me, to make me new.

ON ASCENSION DAY

On that first Ascension Day,
hearts were hurting for minds were confused.
Thinking was all over the place
and souls were profoundly disturbed.

What was he doing?
Where was he going?
Why was he leaving them alone?

The grief was still raw,
the sense of bereftness was still painful,
the fear for the future was as real
as it was worrying.

They wanted him to stay.
They needed him to remain.
They couldn't begin to imagine
what life would be like with their friend no longer there.

But he ascends
to engage in his rightful purpose and eternal destiny.
He goes to take up his place in heaven above.

And yet, still present with his people on this day and every day;
still present in every place and time;
never deserting, never leaving, never abandoning;
always within and around and beside.

In the stillness now,
let us sense the presence of the living God.
Hear his gentle voice of comfort
if you are troubled.
Feel the warmth of his accepting embrace
if you are lonely or bereaved.
In your mind's eye look at the future
which will come and which awaits you.
Let the peace of the one who is here
fill up your senses and suffuse all your mind.

Time for reflection

Jesus, you never leave us nor forsake us.
You will always be our friend.
For you know how much we need you –
from the beginning of our life's dawning
and even beyond its end.

WAR AND PEACE

Suggested music: 'Sanctus and Hosanna' by Karl Jenkins, from The Armed Man. *Alternatively use your own choice of music to reflect the contrast in moods.*

Voice 1:

In unison with all of creation,
which stands as witness to your genius and invention,
we sing our songs of new birth and gladness,
and worship you, God the midwife of life and love.

Again the earth puts on her Sunday best,
and dresses herself up in finest attire.
Flowers of every colour
unite in their silent celebration of you.
Birds build bedrooms
and sing excitedly as they await the arrival of their children.
Grass grows, rabbits run, lambs leap,
and brides blush at bridegrooms
as hope springs eternal in the love they have found in each other.

The dead time of winter is past.
The lifetime of new living is here.
And all of this is your very own doing,
Lord of Life,
Lord of New Life,
Lord of Hope.

Time for reflection (Play background music, e.g. 'Sanctus and Hosanna')

Voice 2:

But then humanity does its worrying worst.
It wastes and warps the wonder of your world with war.
It devastates and destroys and murders and maims.
It bombs and breaks down and hankers after destruction and death.

Lord, have mercy
Christ, have mercy.
Lord, have mercy.

Time for reflection (Play background music)

Voice 3:

In these desert days of your people's experience –
when our failure to be fully human is so very clear,
when our failure to be even semi-God-like is so obvious
and our unwillingness to trust your method of sweet-talking
means that some are now dicing with death –
better is peace than always war.

Lord, have mercy.
Christ, have mercy.
Lord, have mercy on us all.

Time for reflection (Play background music)

Voice 4:

God, save your people.
Save them from each other.
Save them from themselves.
Give peace in our time,
in our church,
in our world.

YOUTH AND AGE

Imagine the scene at your birth:
your mother's cries,
the blood, sweat and tears,
the moment of birthing and breathing.

(Pause)

And then came the calm after the storm.
Hands to hold you were there,
glad smiles of welcome too;
hearts to hansel and warm blankets of love,
reflecting the love which is God.

That we might always respond to heaven's love,
let us pray to the Spirit of the living God.

Song: 'Spirit of the living God, fall afresh on me' (CH4 619)

Think back to the days when you were very young:
the searching and the growing;
the curiosity and the discovery;
the innocence, the amazement, and all your wondering.
Still held by hands when you cried;
still reassured by smiles when you were scared;
still loved by hearts when you were difficult;
still accepted and forgiven when you were thrawn and objectionable.
And all of this, signs of God's living care.

That we might always respond to heaven's compassion,
let us pray to the Spirit of the living God.

Song: 'Spirit of the living God, fall afresh on me'

Think back to the days of your youth:
the shaping and the developing;
the awkwardness and the embarrassment;
the testing and the experimenting;
the risking, the choosing and the mistakes.

There were hands held out in acceptance when you rebelled;
and other hands when you were unreasonable and did your worst.

That we might always appreciate heaven's acceptance,
let us pray to the Spirit of the living God.

Song: 'Spirit of the living God, fall afresh on me'

Think of who you are now:
not the same person you once were.
In your infancy you were more trusting;
in your maturity you are more suspicious.
In your younger years you were more open;
in your older years you are more guarded.
In your childhood you found yourself thinking the best,
in your adulthood you know you often think your critical worst.

That we may be open to renewal and change,
let us pray to the Spirit of the living God.

Song: 'Spirit of the living God, fall afresh on me'

And think of your future: the great unknown.
How would you like to be?
What would you prefer to be?
Who would you opt to be
if your character and personality could be amended and changed?

In the stillness now,
take time to think of what could be different about you.
Think of the areas and aspects where there is room for improvement.
Give thought to what you might focus on to be a different person.
What is the one thing about yourself that you really ought to try to change?

Time for reflection

Spirit of the living God,
fall afresh on me,
and give me the strength and give me the determination
to work on myself
so that I can become new.
Amen

A PERSONAL CONVERSATION

This intimate, personal reflection needs to be taken at a slow and measured pace.

Song: 'Be still and know that I am God' (CH4 754)

Here is the place with its stillness,
and now is the time when there is calm.
This is a quiet oasis of a place
where we can, for a while, leave the business of living to one side,
and banish the turbulence and stress that we sometimes – often –
know only too well.

This is a valuable time,
for God knows each one of us well.
Heaven is aware of every last one of our personal anxieties:
the things that occupy our thinking
and disturb our equilibrium;
the obstacles and barriers that detract from life and living
in all its richness and fullness and peace.

Here is the place, now is the time.
Christ stands before you
and peace is on his mind.

Breathe easily.
Let the rhythm of your breath be relaxed and gentle.
Feel the muscles releasing their tension
so that your body becomes easy and totally at rest.

Here is the place, now is the time.
Christ stands before you and peace is on his mind.

With every easy breath that you take,
feel the peace of God entering your body;
suffusing your blood;
reaching all cells and tissues;
bringing calmness and a sense of security and well-being
that only the great God of love is able to give.

'Peace, be still,' says Jesus. 'Peace, be still.'
Listen to him whispering these words to you personally
in the here and the now.

(Long pause)

'I am the one who calls you my friend.'
Breathe in the friendship of Jesus now;
the warmth of his goodwill and affirmation of you.
He understands your most pressing concerns.
Tell him, and he will listen to your deepest fear.

(Long pause)

'I am the one whose love never fails,' he says.
'I am always with you, even if you forget me.
Depend on me for I am faithful.
Trust me for I refuse to leave your side.'
And as he says this,
you sense yourself beginning to feel more secure.
As he says it, you sense yourself beginning to feel more confident.
As he says this to you personally,
you know reassurance and your once-troubled heart is calm.

In the past you have experienced the strength of his love,
the faithfulness of his loyalty,
and you have known the blessing of his presence
which has lightened and lifted your spirit.
Again this happens now:
deep inside the darkness is lessening,
dispelled by the light of heaven itself.

(Long pause)

'I am the one who says "Follow me,"' he says.
Tell him now how you will try to do that
by trying to trust what he says;
by leaving the future in God's hands.
Tell him what this might mean for you in daily, practical terms.

(Long pause)

Lord, give me faith to live from day to day.
The future is your gift.
And so, holy Jesus,
most merciful redeemer,
friend and brother,
may we see you more clearly,
love you more dearly,
and follow you more nearly day by day.
Amen

ALL ARE WELCOME

It's Sunday morning, and the weekly service has just finished. Many of the congregation have gone into the hall for the usual tea and coffee. There are a lot of folk milling about: some standing in twos, others sitting together around the green-topped Formica tables in groups of four or five or six. The servers on the rota are busy dashing here and there carrying tea- and coffee-pots. There's a good deal of noise because everybody's blethering away ten to the dozen.

Try to imagine you are there. What's the name of the person who is talking to you now? Maybe it is somebody you've known for a long time. Maybe you are part of one of these groups of old friends who always sit together at the same table every week. Maybe the person you are talking to is on the Session or Congregational Board, or a member of the Guild.

The conversation is about the annual coffee morning and plant sale, due to be held in two weeks' time. It's always a busy event and raises a lot of money for congregational funds. The person you are with is telling you they've potted up eight trays of begonia seedlings, and the sturdy little plants are now coming on nicely in his greenhouse. 'That should add a bob or two to the coffers,' he says. 'They always sell like hotcakes.'

But as you agree, you happen to glance over his shoulder and notice there's a woman standing on her own, holding a cup of tea and eating a Jaffa Cake. You don't know who she is: you've never noticed her in the congregation before. She's obviously a newcomer. Because nobody is talking to her, she's pretending to be intensely interested in the notices pinned up on the wall.

You look round the hall a wee bit further, and surprisingly, you see someone else you've never seen in church before. He too is standing on his own and nobody is talking to him either. He's a young guy: early thirties maybe. He's had all the hair shaved off his head, and he's wearing a green sweatshirt with the word NOW printed on the front.

Your eyes meet, and he's mouthing something to you across the hall. He's trying to tell you something, and from the look on his face, it seems to be very urgent. But of course, because of the noise, you can't make out what he's saying. So he smiles, and nods his head towards the woman who's reading the notices. And then he points to his chest: to the single word printed on his green sweatshirt.

And suddenly it dawns on you. He nods towards her again, and his lips move again, repeating the same sentence as before. And then he points to the printing on his sweat-shirt again.

What are these words he keeps on repeating?
What is he trying to tell you?
What is it he is asking you to do?

Time for reflection

Thanks be to Jesus
whose concern is that all are made welcome and accepted.
Thanks be to Jesus
who has shown us how to do it
in the simplest and most practical of ways.

TO THE POWERLESS YOU CAME

To the powerless you came:
the nothings and the nobodies.
The deaf, the lame, the blind,
the mournful and the grieving,
and the broken-hearted ones too.
You came and you gave them a new name.
You renamed them; redesignated them; revalued them,
for you showed them how they were the children
of the most high God.

And then they had a new song to sing.
So they leapt and danced
and with their tongues shouted for joy,
and told others about their God and King.

We have come to worship you.
We have come knowing you value each one of us.
And we have come bringing our needs,
and the needs of others.
We are your chosen people
and we are here so that you can welcome and affirm us
in our humanity.

We don't have to pretend with you
about the things that trouble us,
the threats that unsettle our equilibrium,
the events that have shocked or saddened us.
We don't have to pretend with you
about our less than perfect relationships
or the things that make us ashamed or feel guilty.

There is honesty
in the intimacy of our conversation with you.
We can confide in you our deepest secrets
and say exactly what we feel,
knowing that you will understand.

Listen to the voice of God.
'Lay down what is past.
Share with me your hurt and your pain.
Let me cuddle you,
for in my embrace is healing and wholeness.
And let us journey together,
for today you are a new person,
and today you can go forward in hope.'

Time of silence

Lay it down.
Let it go.
Step gladly; dance lightly.
A new time with your God is now begun.

THEY TOOK AWAY YOUR RIGHTS

They took away your rights as a human being
and they had the audacity to take away your rights as a God.
They denied you justice and withdrew your freedom.
They squeezed the very breath out of your body
and turned the light out on your living on earth.

But little did they know the ways of heaven.
Little did they know – for back you came
singing, dancing, refusing to die.
Back you came,
and your Spirit, your influence, your power lives on,
bringing lightness, laughter and love.

It is the little people who concern you, isn't it? –
the ones who are ignored, and written off,
and shown no fairness.
We'll pray for them now,
and sometimes those little people are ourselves.

A time of quiet

It's the powerful people who really annoy you, isn't it? –
when they abuse their influence,
and ruthlessly misuse their position;
when they gather to themselves,
and ride roughshod over the folk they believe don't matter.
We'll pray for the powerful people now,
and sometimes that might mean praying for ourselves.

A time of quiet

It's the cruelty you just can't stand, isn't it?
It's the lack of equality that really upsets you.
It's the absence of compassion, and the growth of greed
that drives you to deep despair and makes you cry.
You want us to make a stand against all of that,
and fight for the underdog,
and be bothered about the ill-done to,

and recognise that the wood is always made up
of individual trees.

We'll pray for those who are heartless and cruel,
and those who withhold and won't share,
and those who grind others into the ground.
And we'll be conscious that might mean
praying for ourselves.

A time of quiet

Dry your tears. Don't upset yourself any more.
Clear your throat, and through us
break into the silence of secret conspiracies
which result in poverty and hunger.
Clear your throat again, and through us
shout loudly and bang on tables
and protest against inequality and cheating
and fancy footwork.
And clear your throat a third time
so that we can sing your song of protest and praise:

Heaven's freedom for all!
Heaven's dignity for all!
Heaven's peace for all people on earth!

LET YOUR THOUGHTS WANDER

Be still, and let your thoughts wander:
to the person who is, or who has been,
closest and dearest to you.
Think of their face, the way they smile,
the tone of their voice, the sound of their laughter.
In the quietness now,
let God know how much you have appreciated
the quality of this relationship you have shared,
and how grateful you are
that this person has enriched your living experience
during your time here on the earth.

Time for reflection

Think of somebody else you are very fond of:
perhaps someone in your family;
perhaps a friend or a neighbour or a work colleague.
Think of their shape, their height, their weight,
then think of their character, their nature, their ways.
In the quietness, let God know how much you have enjoyed
sharing your life with that person.
Mention the pleasure you have received in knowing them,
and the sense of satisfaction you have experienced
simply because they have been themselves;
simply because of the person they are.

Time for reflection

And now think of someone
you have had no contact with whatsoever.
Look at the face of that hungry child.
Look at the mother whose breasts have no milk.
Look at the young man injecting a vein.
Look at the woman drinking out of a can.
Look at the grandfather ending his days in a bed.
Look at the rich man exploiting his workers.
Speak to God now.
Ask him to show you what you could do
to establish new relationships
so you can feed the hungry, support the weak,
befriend the lonely, change the hearts of the proud and careless.
For we are God's hands and his feet,
and he depends on us now to share his love
so that our living and the living of others
might be full.

Time for reflection

You are love.
May we live in your love
so your love might be set free,
so your love touches each and liberates all.

IT WOULD NEVER CROSS YOUR MIND

God of this earth and all its people,
it would never cross your mind
to turn a single one away:
not because of faith, or the lack of it;
not because of understanding, or the lack of it;
not because of status or gender or absence of goodness.

You just couldn't do that, could you?
You wouldn't be able to do that, would you?
For you are Love in all its acceptance and all its welcome.
You are Love in all its tenderness and warmth and beauty.

Your heart is bigger than we might ever imagine.
Your arms are wider than we could ever conceive.
Your embrace is never withheld, never limited,
nor hesitant nor grudging nor reluctant.
Your blessing and gracious benediction
are for all who live and breathe on this planet Earth.
We have come with gratitude in our hearts
for all that you are, and all that you mean,
and all you have given to make our life rich.

And it is with honesty we have come here too.
There is nothing we can keep from you,
nothing we can hide from you.
For there is nothing at all about us
that you don't already know and understand.

So then,
this is the time,
here is the place,
now is the moment.
In the silence, speak to our need, whatever that is.
Respond to our concerns, whatever they are.
Give us your peace, if that is what we are asking for.
And let us sense your presence, real and active,
so we can feel safe and wholly wanted and fully secure.

Listen to us when we speak to you.
There are things we need to tell you.
Be patient with us,
be understanding, be kindly to us,
for you know what our experience of living is like,
since you also walked on this earth
in the days before we were even born.

Time of silence

Your blessing is ours.
Your forgiveness is ours.
Your love is ours,
God of heaven, God of earth,
the God we worship and praise.

ONLY ONE SIGNIFICANT WORD

You may want to close your eyes for this since it will probably help you to imagine the situation better.

You're in the house by yourself, just before 6 o'clock one night. You've just had your tea, and are about to settle down to watch the news on the telly when there's a knock at the door. *Och, who's that?* you think to yourself. *I hope it's not somebody collecting for the Lifeboats, or Barnardos, or Christian Aid.*

You go and open the door, and standing outside is a wee lady you've never seen before, and she's got a white envelope in her hand. She's wearing a heavy black winter coat, and a red beret. That's a bit odd at this time of year since it's not that cold yet.

'I'm sorry to disturb you,' she says, 'but I've been asked to bring you this message.' She holds out the envelope, which you notice has your name written on it in big block letters. 'A message for me?' you say. 'Who's it from?' 'Oh, it's from God,' she replies, quite casually, as if she were in the habit of delivering messages from God on a daily basis.

'From God?' you say, as you take the envelope from her, all the time thinking: *She must be one of those Jehovah's Witnesses. Either that or she's not quite right in the head.* So you humour her. 'Well, thank you very much. It was good of you to deliver it.' 'Not at all,' she smiles. 'You're very welcome. Bye for now.' She turns and walks away.

You close the door, and go back into the living room and sit down. It's your name on the front of the envelope, right enough. How could she have known your name?

The envelope is one of those self-seal kind, and you tear it open, and inside there's a yellow sheet of paper, folded once. You unfold it, and see more of the same writing that was on the envelope: clearly it has been written by the same hand. But the strange thing is that there's only one word there: only one word, though it's a very significant word – very significant to you, that is, for the word describes a real issue in your life at this time.

A message from God, and all summed up in this one word on the yellow sheet of paper.

- What is that word?
- And what could God possibly be saying to you about it?
- What is this message from heaven you're supposed to understand?
- And what is it that God wants you to know by sending an angel to your front door?

Time for reflection

God, help us to see your presence
everywhere we look and in everyone we look at.
Help us to understand you are always intimately involved
and passionately concerned
with everything and all that happens in our lives.

A SPECIAL MOMENT

Voice 1:

This is a special moment:
a time to be intimate with you.
Here is when we come very close to you,
and now is when you come close to us.

You live in our minds whenever we give you space.
You live in our heartbeats
when we choose to mention your name.
You live in our souls,
the deepest and most crucial parts of our being,
and there you give healing,
and there you give mending
and there you give peace.

So then, Great Love,
we give you a chance to work within us now.
We give you a chance to inspire us,
and plant seeds of new life in who we are.

Voice 2:

Relationships have gone wrong,
trust has been betrayed,
love has grown cold,
and those who love us have been hurt.
Speak now, and we will listen to what you say.

A time of silence

Voice 1:

There is grieving,
there is isolation,
there is loneliness.
People we know and people we don't know
are unhappy and anxious.
Some are disturbed
and hope has all but disappeared.
Speak now, and we will listen carefully.
Speak now, and tell us what we should do
to help give them peace.

A time of silence

Voice 2:

There is unfairness,
there is power-seeking,
there is apathy and avarice.
And not everyone cares,
and not everyone listens,
and fewer still will act.
Speak now, and we will listen carefully.
Speak now, and tell us clearly
what you want us to do.

A time of silence

Voice 1:

God use us and God inspire us.
God encourage us, and God give us energy
to be Christ's hands, to love one another
so his kingdom might come.

AT THE END OF THE DAY

Song: 'Lord of life, we come to you' (CH4 782) (effective if sung by an unaccompanied solo voice)

Voice 1:

At the end of the day, we gather with you.
At the end of the day, when minds are dull
and bones are tired, we meet with you.
At the end of the day, when hearts are tender,
and souls are open, and heaven is near,
Lord of Life, we come to you.

Song: 'Lord of life, we come to you'

Voice 2:

We have come to find comfort.

Voice 3:

We have come to find challenge.

Voice 2:

We have come expecting nothing.

Voice 3:

We have come feeling insecure.

Voice 2:

We have come feeling happy.

Voice 3:

We have come to sing.

Voice 2:

We have come to feel your love.

Voice 3:

We have come, as others have also come.

Voice 1:

Lord of Life, we come to you.

Song: 'Lord of life, we come to you'

Voice 2:

We need to know you accept us.

Voice 3:

We need to hear your words: 'Well done!'

Voice 2:

We need to sense and know the power of your forgiveness.

Voice 3:

We need to hear your words: 'I keep no record.'

Voice 2:

We need to hear your voice saying: 'You are mine.'

Voice 1:

Lord of Life, we come to you.

Song: 'Lord of life, we come to you'

Voice 3:

In the mystery of your presence
no words are needed.

Voice 2:

In the depth of your silence
no words are needed.

Voice 3:

In the intimacy of your nearness
no words are needed.

Voice 1:

You are here.
You are with us.
We will be still.

Time of reflection

Song: 'Lord of life, we come to you'

Voice 1:

With the light of your love you fascinate us.

Voice 2:

Through the light of your love you heal us.

Voice 3:

By the light of your love you change us.

Voice 1:

In the light of your love, we are free to move on.

LET US BE STILL

Voice 1:

Let us be still, and in the silence
give thanks for the heritage of faith
that has been celebrated in this place for so long:

for the way our ancestors helped to shape the world around them,
having met their God here time and again;

for those who have worked hard,
and still work hard, for their church and God
because their passion and enthusiasm
is that the kingdom of heaven should be built more quickly
here on the earth.

Let us be still and give thanks for all of that.

A time of silence

Voice 2:

Let us be still, and in the silence
thank God for our own personal journey
which we have made over so many years:
for the ways in which the Powerful One
has influenced and changed us as individuals;

for the difference that has made
in other people's lives;

for the sense of heaven's hand
which has guided and steered us;

for Christ's Body, his living Church,
of which we have been privileged to be a part.

Let us be still and give thanks to God for all of that.

A time of silence

Voice 3:

Let us be still, and in the silence
ask God whether, through us,
he will heal and mend others who are hurting and broken
as we do our living in the week that is to come.

Voice 1:

In the silence, we will mention to God
the name of the person who is grieving.
Will the Compassionate One want us to go
and give comfort and friendship on his behalf?

Voice 2:

In the silence, we will mention to God
the name of the person who is needy, or unpopular,
or particularly awkward to deal with.
Will the Accepting One want us to go
and make a point of letting them know they are loved?

Voice 3:

In the silence, we will mention to God
the name of the person who is unhappy,
or afraid, or insecure, or isolated and lonely.
Will the Understanding One want us to go
and listen to how they feel,
and share in the story of their anxiety,
and give our company,
and give our time,
and give our love?

Voice 1:

In the silence, we will be still.
In the silence we will pray that the work of heaven
is carried out on the earth.

A time of silence

Voice 2:

God of this place and time,
God of every place and time,
make prayer my work,
make work my prayer
so that your healing is real.

IF WE SAID YOU WERE WONDERFUL

Voice 1:

If we said you were wonderful,
that wouldn't be enough.
If we claimed you are powerful,
that would be to sell you short.
If we said there is nothing and no one greater than you,
then maybe we'd be getting closer to the mark.

Voice 2:

You spoke your Word, and this world was.

Voice 3:

Then you loved your people into being:
made for love; made in love; made by Love itself.

Voice 1:

And you have called us here.
You know how many freckles are on our face,
the shade of our hair, the length of our fingers.
And you decided on the colour of our eyes.

Voice 2:

You know the looks we can give;
the gestures of encouragement or disapproval we make;
the way we show our anger; the sound of our laughter;
the way that we dance.

Voice 3:

You know the tone of our voice;
the mood of our minds; the secrets of our hearts.
For each of us is a brand-new adventure
in your spectacular imagination.

Voice 1:

So then – celebrated wildly in heaven
from the moment of our conception,
with excited angels clapping their hands
and smiling with joy –
made in heaven, made for heaven,
made to live on the earth: the children of God.

Voice 2:

God, look kindly on us
when we treat each other like strangers and not friends.

Voice 3:

Pardon our bigotry, our prejudices,
our feelings of superiority and smugness.

Voice 1:

Give us forgiveness if we know we have
not looked for signs of your presence in those who surround us,
and settle our minds if, in our fear and in our doubting,
we contemplate a future in which you may be absent.

Voice 2:

God you made me and you know me.
Give me your attention now.
Listen to my voice,
and I will tell you about what I feel at this time.

Time of silence

Voice 3:

You are a good God, a merciful God.
You hold no record
and your forgiveness is total and complete.

Voice 1:

Glory to God in highest heaven!

Voice 2:

He is ours.

Voice 3:

We are his.

Voices 1, 2, 3:

Our living is secure.
Amen

MUSIC SOURCES

Church Hymnary, Fourth Edition (CH4), Canterbury Press, 2005

Come All You People: Shorter Songs for Worship from the Iona Community, John L. Bell, Wild Goose Publications, 1994, 2010

Common Ground: A Song Book for all the Churches (CG), St Andrew Press, 1998

Enemy of Apathy: Wild Goose Songs, Volume 2 – Songs of the Passion and Resurrection of Jesus, and the Coming of the Holy Spirit, John L. Bell & Graham Maule, Wild Goose Publications, 1988, revised 1990

Love from Below: Wild Goose Songs, Volume 3 – The Seasons of Life, the Call to Care, and Celebrating Community, 1989, 1998, John L. Bell, Wild Goose Publications

Many and Great: Songs of the World Church, Volume 1, edited and arranged by John L. Bell, Wild Goose Publications, 1990

The Courage to Say No: Twenty-three Songs for Lent and Easter, John L. Bell & Graham Maule, Wild Goose Publications, 1996

There Is One Among Us: Shorter Songs for Worship, John L. Bell, Wild Goose Publications, 1998